365 DAILY DEVOTIONS

IN JESUS' NAME
FOR
Men

BroadStreet
PUBLISHING

BroadStreet Publishing Group, LLC.
Savage, Minnesota, USA
Broadstreetpublishing.com

IN JESUS' NAME FOR MEN

© 2023 by BroadStreet Publishing®

9781424566433
9781424566440 (eBook)

Prayers composed by Eoghan Holdahl.

Typesetting and design by Garborg Design Works | garborgdesign.com
Editorial services by Michelle Winger | literallyprecise.com

Printed in China.

23 24 25 26 27 28 29 7 6 5 4 3 2 1

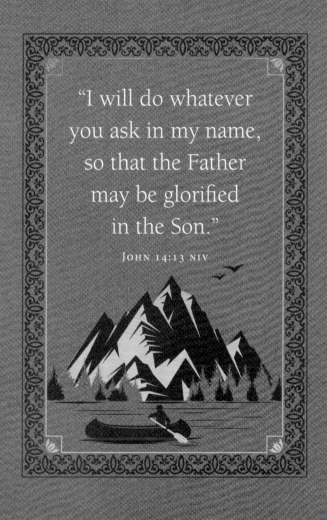

"I will do whatever you ask in my name, so that the Father may be glorified in the Son."

John 14:13 NIV

Introduction

Jesus said we can do all that he did in his ministry on earth and even more if we believe in him. This is no small statement! Jesus performed large displays of God's power through miracles, signs, and wonders. We were never meant to stay small in prayer or in faith. When Jesus said *whatever you ask*, it included the big, bold prayers that would be impossible to accomplish on our own.

As you read these Scriptures, short devotions, and prayers, pray in Jesus' name with faith! Take him at his word and ask for greater things. Grow bold in the way you ask him to move in your life and in the world around you. He loves to save, heal, comfort, and amaze.

We catch a glimpse of the glory and goodness of God through answered prayer. He has not stopped moving in power, so let's keep asking him to show up in wonderful ways.

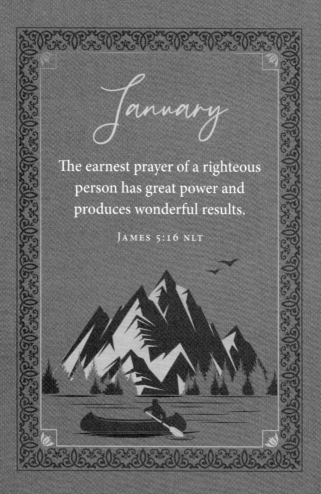

January

The earnest prayer of a righteous
person has great power and
produces wonderful results.

James 5:16 nlt

Sing Praise

It is good to give thanks to the LORD,
to sing praises to the Most High.
It is good to proclaim your unfailing love in the morning,
your faithfulness in the evening.

PSALM 92:1-2 NLT

Without an agenda, give thanks to the Lord today. How has he been good to you? How have you witnessed his strong mercy in your life? Pour out your praises to him. Let your heart swell with wonder as you remember how faithful he has been. His unfailing love has not left you yet, and it never will. Proclaim it over your day, your family, your life. His unfailing love covers you all the days of your life.

Thank you, Jesus, for everything you have blessed me with. Your mercy has been evident in my life from my first breath, and it will continue to remain until my last. You have always been faithful to me, and I am so grateful for your unfailing love. I praise you today because you are worthy of being praised with my every breath.

All Generations

This forever-song I sing of the gentle love of God!
Young and old alike will hear about
your faithful, steadfast love—never failing!

PSALM 89:1 TPT

God is constant in compassion, and full of second chances.
In fact, he doesn't put a limit on his mercy at all. It is never
failing, never ending, and powerful to save. Why would we
hide our joy when he is the pure delight of our lives? He is
too marvelous for words, yet we shouldn't stop declaring his
goodness to all who will listen.

*Jesus, I will sing about your goodness. The song of my heart
overflows to the melody on my lips. You are full of love that
never ends. Your everlasting kindness is my assurance and
my strength. You do not leave even one of your loved ones
behind. You are the God who leaves the ninety-nine on the
path of life to rescue the one who has gone astray.*

Big List

Let all that I am praise the LORD;
with my whole heart, I will praise his holy name.
Let all that I am praise the LORD;
may I never forget the good things he does for me.

PSALM 103:1-2 NLT

The person who wrote this Bible verse was thankful for everything that God had given him. He was thankful for little things like flowers, surprise gifts, and quiet mornings, as well as big things like healing, relationships, and forgiveness of sin. Remember to praise God for all these wonderful things today.

Oh Lord in heaven, I will praise you this day. With all my heart, all my mind, and all my soul, I will raise up my praises to you in everlasting thanksgiving. Nothing compares to having you on my side; I will not forget this.

A Changed Heart

"I say to you, love your enemies.
Pray for those who hurt you."

MATTHEW 5:44 NCV

It is not easy to love your enemies. Jesus did not command that we tolerate our enemies or peacefully avoid them, but that we actually change our hearts to love them. The way we can do this is by actively praying for them. When we genuinely pray to God, our hearts begin to soften and change. We are invested in that for which we are praying. We were Christ's enemies when we were outside of grace. He suffered the cross for our sake because he loves us. Now, in response to that unimaginable love, we are told to love others including our enemies.

Jesus, in light of the great love you have shown me, I will display love to those around me. I will love those who hurt me and those who are enemies of the cross. Just as you advocated for my soul, I will advocate for those who hurt me.

Clear Guide

The Lord has told you what is good,
and this is what he requires of you:
to do what is right, to love mercy,
and to walk humbly with your God.

MICAH 6:8 NLT

Fortunately, as Christians, we don't have to question what God requires of us. He has written it in the Bible. We have a plan book that shows us the way and gives us specific instructions on how to live right, love mercy, and walk with God. Any time we question the right thing for us to do, we can search the Scriptures and find the answer.

Dear Lord, no matter where I am in life, I pray that I would continue to measure my conduct by the standard you set. Not by man's standards, or by my own, but by yours, Lord. You are righteous, seeking for children of mercy, humility, and righteousness. May I be counted among them.

A Delicate Balance

*Set your minds on the things that are above,
not on the things that are on earth.*

COLOSSIANS 3:2 NASB

Isn't creation incredible? Isn't God's handiwork infinitely glorious? Our world is dazzling in its beauty, bursting with opportunity, and dizzying in its variety. It's also a tremendous distraction. We can get so caught up in our own possessions and problems, and in the vast wonders God supplied to the earth, we fail to remember the Supplier. Instead of being grateful for our homes, we become proud and possessive. The purpose we get from our worldly tasks can morph into obsession. Treating our bodies with respect can veer us into vanity. Remember, none of these earthly things define us. Only the Lord does that. Let him, and his love, be all that consumes us.

Heaven is my home, oh Lord. Only heaven can give me the peace I require. I will fix my eyes on your place of eternity, casting aside the distractions and idols that claw for my heart. There is nothing, Jesus, that can take the place you have in my mind and give me what you give.

Description of Glory

All around him was a glowing halo, like a rainbow shining in
the clouds on a rainy day. This is what the glory of the LORD
looked like to me. When I saw it, I fell face down on the
ground, and I heard someone's voice speaking to me.

EZEKIEL 1:28 NLT

When we finally meet Jesus face to face, we might have a
different way to describe what he looks like, but Ezekiel's
description is pretty magnificent. The human language is
limited, yet we need to appreciate the beauty of descriptions.
It is true that Jesus is our hope for the future; he is like that
promise represented by a rainbow on a rainy day. Yes, he is
our friend, but he is also the King of kings, and he is worthy
to be worshipped.

*You alone, Lord God, are perfect in both humility and
majesty. Fully man and fully divine, you are the perfection
of every good thing. I rely on you, and I glorify you for the
greatness of your character.*

A Gift

LORD, every morning you hear my voice.
Every morning, I tell you what I need,
and I wait for your answer.

PSALM 5:3 NCV

Every time our sun has moved its way over the horizon
line into our skies, it can be defined as one thing: a gift. It
doesn't matter what season it is, or if those skies are cloudy,
full of storms, crystal clear, or speckled with fluffy white
marshmallows. When our eyes flutter upon that first light,
God himself is there holding the gift. Anticipation is full. Let
the beauty of this sink into your heart for a moment. The
God of the universe is presenting you with extraordinary
gifts. What do you need?

*Apart from you, what is there for me to desire, Lord? You are
the fullness of every blessing, the essence of every good thing.
I have only to confide in you, and you fill my every need and
listen to my desires.*

Good Father

> "Don't worry. For your Father cares deeply
> about even the smallest detail of your life."
>
> MATTHEW 10:30-31 TPT

Worry is a thief, and this generation is being robbed blind. Do you realize what is being stolen from you? The smallest moments as a whole make up your life. When you succumb to worry, you lose your life. But you do not have to live in the poverty of worry. You serve an all-powerful, all-knowing God who cares so deeply for those small moments. He wants to tend to the moments that are being stolen by anxiety and redeem them. He can change all those circumstances that are haunting you.

Amid this sea of life's cares, you are my vessel, Lord. You alone keep me from drowning in my anxiety, and you sustain me through all the trials and difficult details. Please, Jesus, help me to trust in you more fully this day.

King's Dream

Daniel replied, "There are no wise men, enchanters, magicians, or fortune-tellers who can reveal the king's secret. But there is a God in heaven who reveals secrets, and he has shown King Nebuchadnezzar what will happen in the future. Now I will tell you your dream and the visions you saw as you lay on your bed."

DANIEL 2:27-28 NLT

Daniel could have presented himself as some kind of skillful mind reader, but he gave all the glory to God. He could have used his gift of interpretation to make himself great in the king's palace, but with sincerity of heart he directed the king toward the one true God who knows all things. There are times when you might be tempted to take the glory for yourself. Remember who gave you your gifts and allow your accomplishments to point toward the magnificence of your God.

Lord, you alone deserve all the glory. There is no other God in heaven but you, and nothing else deserves my worship. No one else can read the hearts of men and the future. Help me to give you the glory on this day.

Written Words

As soon as I pray, you answer me;
you encourage me by giving me strength.
Every king in all the earth will thank you, LORD,
for all of them will hear your words.

PSALM 138:3-4 NLT

The written word is mostly digital these days which makes it very efficient to get your thoughts down. But there is something almost sacred about using your hands to write—the way scribes would have done for the kings. Consider this Psalm and how you might have written a prayer of gratitude. What, or who, do you have to be thankful for in your life?

Lord, thank you for being close. Your strength sustains me in times of need, and you have shown yourself to be enough in all times. Truly all kings and rulers will bow one day before your throne and give you the glory you deserve.

Unique Song

He put a new song in my mouth,
a song of praise to our God.

PSALM 40:3 ESV

Since the beginning of time, songs have been written. One could assume that every topic has been covered: sorrow, heartache, hope, joy, healing—the list goes on. With the millions of songs written, could there truly be a new song? God's knowledge and wisdom are unmeasurable, and no created being will ever fully grasp the depth of his persona even if they have walked with him for their entire life. There is always something new to sing about him!

When I am bored and feel a lull in my spiritual life, please remind me of your brilliance, God. Reveal to me again a glimpse of your glory, so that I would not forget just how incomparable you are in goodness and grace.

A New Thing

"Behold, I am doing a new thing;
now it springs forth, do you not perceive it?
I will make a way in the wilderness
and rivers in the desert."

ISAIAH 43:19 ESV

The prophet Isaiah recorded many of God's reminders to the people of Israel. They readily forgot his miracles and abandoned his ways, so he constantly reminded them of who he was and what he had done for them, proving that he was worthy of their praise and worship. When we were all lost to sin with no hope of redemption, God sent his Son, Jesus Christ, to make a way for us: a way in the wilderness. This is the "new thing" he was doing.

Dear Lord, please use this day to remind me of your faithfulness. When I have lost my way, and when I feel broken, remind me that you are still sovereign. No authority compares to yours, so please help me to have faith.

Risk Taker

> Your word is a lamp to guide my feet
> and a light for my path.
> PSALM 119:105 NLT

There will be opportunities that arise that might be surprising to us. We might suddenly be presented with something that feels kind of terrifying. We view it as an opportunity because we see the benefit in it somewhere along the way. Stepping through the unknown takes courage, and courage isn't always readily available. Through the power of prayer, we come to the point where our hearts feel the peace we've been looking for. That makes the task of accepting the opportunity much easier.

This world is full of darkness, Jesus, so please be the light of my world. Illuminate the way when I have doubts and bring me peace when there is chaos around me. Nothing compares to the radiance of your truth. Please illuminate my path.

Song of David

My heart is confident in you, O God;
no wonder I can sing your praises with all my heart!

PSALM 108:1 NLT

The Psalms communicate the highs and lows of life: the mountaintops and valleys. This Psalm is a mountaintop moment. These are the moments you feel self-assured, confident of what lies ahead, and optimistic for the future—you almost boast about it! Embrace these moments and celebrate with enthusiasm. If you can't celebrate for yourself today, celebrate for someone else.

In the highs and the lows, you are still God. You are sovereign, and you remain steadfast. My world may be shaking, but you are not. You are unshakeable, and I am confident in you.

Warm Welcome

Accept one another, then,
just as Christ accepted you,
in order to bring praise to God.

ROMANS 15:7 NIV

Have you ever met someone and immediately felt a connection? Maybe you were drawn to their personality and a friendship was born. We all have our natural friendships. We don't have to be best friends with everyone we meet because the truth of it is, we won't be. But what if, despite our differences, we still accepted all those we come in contact with?

Jesus, why do I reject others, when I myself cannot live without your unconditional acceptance? Am I perfect, Jesus, that I should cast judgement on others? Help me today to bless and not to curse.

A Way Out

How long must I struggle with anguish in my soul,
with sorrow in my heart every day?
How long will my enemy have the upper hand?

PSALM 13:2 NLT

One of the hardest realities of life is that we can't escape suffering. There is no easy fix to a heart or mind that has been broken or wounded in some way. You may be able to relate to an experience where you have felt sorrow in your heart every day. During those times of struggle, you desperately want a way out. It's important to cry out to God and acknowledge that you are totally dependent on him for help. Keep hoping and praying; he is a God that can be trusted.

I can trust you, God, with the truth of how I feel. I will not hide my pain or my anguish from you any longer, but I will lay it bare for you to see so I might find healing.

Abba

You did not receive a spirit of slavery to fall back into fear.
Instead, you received the Spirit of adoption, by whom we cry
out, "Abba, Father!" The Spirit himself testifies together with
our spirit that we are God's children.

ROMANS 8:15-16 CSB

Abba. It's the Aramaic word used for Father. Used by
children and adults alike, the word drips with intimacy.
Using it shows familiarity, vulnerability, and a deep sense of
trust. Do these words seem foreign to you when referring
to God? Some of us grew up with very rigid fathers:
relationships void of the words above. Others grew up in a
stoic and rigid religion, without the warm familiarity of a
loving, kind father. By simply saying in prayer, "My Father!"
the Holy Spirit unlocks a level of intimacy with God. Try
praying this way, and rest in the care you receive from your
loving, kind Father.

*Father, how great it is to be adopted into your family! I
praise you for giving me the privilege of being in your family.
I thank you for your warm embrace.*

Abundance Follows

Good planning and hard work lead to prosperity,
but hasty shortcuts lead to poverty.

PROVERBS 21:5 NLT

If lists, calendars, and flowcharts rule our days, verses like this one are great news. If we love making plans, it's affirming to read that it's pleasing to God and leads us to prosperity. However, plan with care. Without prayer and remaining close to God's will, we can run ahead of him—and end up lost.

Dear God, I know that unless you build the house, those who build it build in vain. I render my life to you, so that through my planning and your sovereign hand it would be built for your glory.

Acceptable Speech

Let the words of my mouth
and the meditation of my heart
be acceptable to you,
O Lord, my rock and my redeemer.

PSALM 19:14 ESV

The words that come out of our mouths are influenced by the motives which are hidden in our hearts. What we focus our time on will be what flows in our conversation. We ought to remember the Lord who authored our creation, salvation, and preservation. It is he alone who redeemed us through his death and resurrection, and it is he alone who sustains us by his power and might.

I need your grace to purify my soul, Jesus! Without you, the very meditation of my heart and the contents of my mind are fruitless. Please sustain me today in my thoughts.

Alert Mind

Devote yourselves to prayer
with an alert mind and a thankful heart.
COLOSSIANS 4:2 NLT

Prayer does not require the perfect sentiments or a specific style. It is an open door of communication between us and heaven. Prayer is bigger than a statement we make in churches or cathedrals. It is more than a request we make in desperation. It can be as constant as our breathing. When we devote ourselves to prayer, we can do it with intention and thanksgiving. We know Jesus is full of mercy, and we can expect to be met by his love every time we turn to him.

Jesus, my prayer today is that this would not be my only prayer. My prayer is that you would fill my mind and heart with prayer throughout the day, from sunrise to sunset, so I might live in your glory.

All About God

For out of him, the sustainer of everything, came everything, and now everything finds fulfillment in him. May all praise and honor be given to him forever! Amen!

ROMANS 11:36 TPT

Having eyes for the kingdom of God will make you feel like an outsider in the world. We should expect to be hated by the world, but there will even be those who call themselves believers who find you to be too much. A life dedicated to the glory of God is never too much. A heart set on seeking him is exactly where it needs to be. A mouth proclaiming his goodness and mercy so that the rocks don't cry out is saying what needs to be said. A mind set on the Spirit is to be commended.

Not to me, Lord, but to you is all the glory due! I live only to be found pleasing to you, and to be enlivened by your love. You have created and sustained me, so I glorify you for your power and rule.

Another View

We give thanks to God always for all of you,
constantly mentioning you in our prayers.

1 THESSALONIANS 1:2 ESV

Have you been stuck in a conversation with someone
who only talks about themselves? Every word out of their
mouth is centered around their view of the world and how
everything affects them. It's difficult to relate because there is
plenty of talking but no listening. It's a one-way street. Let's
not allow our prayers to be all one-way. Prayer is a beautiful
gift. We can communicate with the God of the universe!

*God, I pray over those I have seen shining your light in a
dark world. I rejoice over them and pray that you would
continue to do a good work through them. Thank you, Jesus,
for what you are doing!*

For Jesus

Whatever you do in word or deed,
do all in the name of the Lord Jesus,
giving thanks through Him to God the Father.

COLOSSIANS 3:17 NASB

When we focus on what people around us expect, we can become burnt out and resentful that we are being stretched thin. Instead of complaining or grumbling to ourselves while doing chores around the house, going out of our way to meet a friend, or doing a task that we wish others would do, let's approach it as if we were doing it for God. He sees what others miss.

All my life I have been blessed, Father, and I pray that my lips would bless you this day in thankfulness. I thank you for your grace, and I thank you for the cross.

All Our Praise

They sang a new song, saying, "Worthy are you to take the
scroll and to open its seals, for you were slain, and by your
blood you ransomed people for God from every tribe and
language and people and nation."

REVELATION 5:9 ESV

Jesus is the worthy one, the King of kings and Lord of lords.
Every tribe, every language, every people, and every nation
are offered the same power of his redemption. We are all
as one in Christ, and none of us has a better claim to come
before him than any other. May we join with heaven in
proclaiming Jesus as King over all. He is worthy of all our
lives, all our praise, and all our honor. There are no tiers in
his family. May we be unified in love.

*You alone, Jesus, are worthy to open the scroll! You alone
stand resurrected from a penalty you did not deserve, and
you alone deserve to be lifted up. Thank you, Jesus, for being
my King!*

Lovely Things

All praise to God, the Father of our Lord Jesus Christ.
God is our merciful Father and the source of all comfort.

2 CORINTHIANS 1:3 NLT

The lovely things of life—sunsets, fresh fruit, warmth, spring
water—they are all created by God to glorify him. He clothed
the world in beauty to be pleasing in his sight. Although
we live in a broken version of the original Eden, we catch
glimpses of the earth that God has planned for the future. If
we look, we can see signs of a coming new earth even in our
everyday lives, truly good things that give us hope for the
time to come.

Even the grass glorifies you. I am surrounded by a world,
God, that testifies to your comfort and mercy. As long as
there is air in my lungs, I pray that I would glorify you for it.

All Praise

Praise the LORD in song, for He has done excellent things;
let this be known throughout the earth.

ISAIAH 12:5 NASB

Our God is so worthy! All praise, respect, honor, and glory belong with him. Amazed by talent, let us glorify the One who formed the hands that did the painting. Let us lift up the Father of the voice who sang the song. Beholding beauty, let us sing of the glorious mind who imagined, then spoke it into being. Every time we are dazzled, let our hearts remember our God, who designs, creates, and blesses us with it all, and let us not be shy in giving him the credit. As long as we have breath, let us spend it honoring the one who gives it.

All my honor is due to you, God, and to none other. My mind is filled by the excellency of your testimony, and I pray that my praise would reach to the ends of the earth. I will certainly proclaim your mercies this day!

What Is Within

Bless the LORD, O my soul,
and all that is within me,
bless his holy name!
Bless the LORD, O my soul,
and forget not all his benefits.

PSALM 103:1-2 ESV

We can choose to bless the Lord, to offer him praise and thanks no matter what we are feeling in the moment. We can choose to focus on what he has given, and how fellowship with him has enriched our lives. No matter how we feel at any given moment, we can turn our attention to focusing on all the ways that we have been blessed by God.

Lord, thank you for your abundant mercy and your shower of benefits! Thank you for washing away every sin and making me righteous in you. May everything within me and all those around me praise your glorious name.

Always Near

> "When you walk through the fire of oppression,
> you will not be burned up; the flames will not consume you.
> For I am the LORD, your God, the Holy One of Israel,
> your Savior."
>
> ISAIAH 43:2-3 NLT

You serve an ever-present God. He is always with you. When your emotions are frazzled, he is with you. When you feel swallowed up in disappointment, you will not drown. When you experience trauma, it will not consume you. His promises are good and true, and he promises to always uphold you. What are the deep waters that you are wading through right now? Trust that he is near you. He has not left you alone to navigate treacherous waters. He sees you, knows you, and longs to meet you exactly where you are.

Jesus, it is in you that I place my trust. I rely on your promises and pray for you to deliver me at every step in this life. Thank you for not giving me over to the fiery flames of destruction, but instead rescuing my soul from the pit.

Ready

Pray in the Spirit at all times with all kinds of prayers, asking
for everything you need. To do this you must always be
ready and never give up. Always pray for all God's people.

EPHESIANS 6:18 NCV

When we live with surrendered hearts to God and an open
line of communication, we will always be ready to pray. In
every circumstance, every challenging situation, and every
season of calm, we can present our pleas to God. Even when
our lives are at rest, there will be others walking through
the fire of testing. May we pray with compassion and fierce
faith on their behalf. When you are at a loss, Jesus never is.
Partner with him in prayer and see how your faith grows.

May I learn to pray to you in the Spirit at all times, Jehovah.
May I learn to trust you with my stray thoughts, to give
you my every care, and to not let this life be the focus of my
heart. Be the focus of my heart.

Type of Joy

Rejoice in the Lord always.
I will say it again: Rejoice!

PHILIPPIANS 4:4 NIV

Joy is a great gift from God. It is far more powerful than happiness because it does not diminish due to circumstances. The type of joy that God gives does not come from this world; therefore, it is not dependent on this world. No enemy can steal it and no disappointment can drown it out. It should define our personalities and be ever in our hearts. Understanding what God has done for us will fill us with joy and it will be obvious to those around us. Even when we are sad, God's joy is still in our hearts, and it compels us forward.

For a thousand reasons, Lord, I will praise your name this day! I will delight in you, rejoice in you, and partake of you this day. May my every sorrow be turned to dancing, and my song be one of delight in you.

February

Look to the Lᴏʀᴅ and his strength;
seek his face always.

1 Chʀᴏɴɪᴄʟᴇs 16:11 ɴɪᴠ

Answers

When I was in trouble, I called to the LORD,
and he answered me.

PSALM 120:1 NCV

It does not matter how small, how big, how complex, or how simple your troubles are; God will help you with them all. Don't hold back your prayers or requests from him. Don't hesitate to call on him in everything. He is a loving father and a willing help. Call on him with confidence not only for your soul but also for your circumstances. He is a ready and strong advocate who will rise up on your behalf.

On my behalf, Lord, you will surely rise up. You will not leave me to fight these battles alone but will be my vanguard and my rearguard, hedging me in safely on every side. Teach me to call to you in times of need, so I would see your providential hand.

Prayer and Peace

Do not be anxious about anything, but in everything by prayer and supplication with thanksgiving let your requests be made known to God. And the peace of God, which surpasses all understanding, will guard your hearts and your minds in Christ Jesus.

PHILIPPIANS 4:6-7 ESV

Prayer is the means by which we overcome our anxieties. We don't always know what the result will be, but God is in control and has our best interests at heart. If we have truly released the burden of our anxieties and fears to the Lord, our hearts will be protected by the peace of God. His peace protects our minds from running to every possible scenario. It often doesn't make sense that we should be at peace in the midst of distressing circumstances, so when we are, we can be assured that peace came from God.

Rather than seeking out coping mechanisms today, Lord, may I find my peace in you. Help me to see beyond all the reasons for anxiety, so I would see you as the answer to it all. Fill me with your peace this day.

Anxious Hearts

"Seek first the kingdom of God and His righteousness, and all these things shall be added to you. Therefore do not worry about tomorrow, for tomorrow will worry about its own things."

MATTHEW 6:33–34 NKJV

The desires of our heart can constantly be at odds with the desires God has for us. When they align, it is a beautiful, peaceful realization. But when they are different, it can create confusion, mistrust, and frustration—often because we lack discernment. So we pray. We pray that God gives us peace. We pray that his will be done no matter what that means for us. In strict obedience to God, we choose not to be anxious. He promises to guard our hearts. If we start to feel frustrated or anxious again, we pray. So much of life is out of our control, so why do we bother agonizing? We should just pray.

Above all the needs I see, Lord, I place the duty of your kingdom. May it direct my steps, informing how I complete all of life's task. With you as my shining goal, I know there is no reason for worry.

Applause

Better to be patient than powerful;
better to have self-control than conquer a city.

PROVERBS 16:32 NLT

Social media gives us the ability to look over the sea of humanity and see highlight reels from people's lives. We fall into the trap of comparing ourselves to others. We look out and see our friends building empires and conquering dreams. To help fight the comparison trap, which kills our courage and seizes us with fear, a key principle needs to be remembered. In God's kingdom, your heart is what matters. That means it is better to be unseen and growing the fruit of the Spirit than to be applauded by the masses.

Dear Jesus, rather than seeking the recognition of men, may I seek your approbation. May I seek the glory of being called your child above every honor and prestige. Please create in me your eternal image of glory.

Appreciated

I praise you because you remember me in everything, and you follow closely the teachings just as I gave them to you.

1 CORINTHIANS 11:2 NCV

This Scripture clarifies what it means to appreciate and be appreciated with mutual gratitude. One of the greatest gifts to show appreciation for someone can be taking what they taught you and replicating it. People recognize the original source and are pleased by it. Another manner of appreciation is expressing gratitude for something someone has done. Paul writes here how he cherishes that the Corinthian church has taken to heart his teaching, respected what he said, and faithfully lived it out. This is mutual appreciation at its best!

Dear God, please teach me this day to show appreciation for those around me. May their sense of value be informed by my kind words toward them, and may I be a source of hope for them.

Bump in the Road

O God in Zion, to you even silence is praise!
You who answers prayer;
all of humanity comes before you with their requests.

PSALM 65:2 TPT

We hit a bump in the road and really need a favor. We
wrestle with who to turn to. We have friends we could
approach and family members who would step in, but they
would ask, "How did you get yourself into this mess?" They
may agree to give us some support but also lecture us about
what we might have done differently. We never need to be
concerned about coming to God with any request. We don't
have to stress over whether he will listen or think our need
is silly. We will never be turned away; he welcomes us with
open arms.

*Lord, today I come to you with a request. Humble me, so I
would know that I must always bring my requests to you.
Help me stop trying to fulfill all my requests myself. Surely
this is vanity.*

Approaching God

This is the confidence we have in approaching God:
that if we ask anything according to his will, he hears us.

1 JOHN 5:14 NIV

This verse should vanquish any idea Christians may have of God simply being a wishing well. Tossing prayers up to heaven and hoping for our own desires to be fulfilled is not how lovestruck, servant-hearted believers are expected to approach the Almighty. When our deepest desire is for the Lord and for all people to come to know him, we pray to him for directions and answers that align with his agenda. That does not mean we have to vet our prayers or leave out details and requests that matter to us, but that everything comes under a covering of a mutual understanding that his master plan is what we are aiming at and hoping for above all else.

God, today please teach me to ask according to your will. There is much I could ask for which I do not need, so I pray you would teach me to ask for what you want. Thank you for the confidence I have in approaching you!

Ark of Strength

Arise, LORD, to Your resting place,
You and the ark of Your strength.

PSALM 132:8 NASB

David was a keen worshipper, but he also had a great reason to dance! The ark of the covenant was back in his possession, and having the Lord's presence with him meant that God's favor was present. David had a huge reason to celebrate, and so do we! The presence of God is with us—he is in our hearts—and that means his favor is too. Dance before the Lord like no one is watching today! Celebrations are part of our faith; they remind us of the goodness of God.

God of strength and might, how could I ever search for security in myself? Surely it is only you who give strength, and it is only you who can empower me. Please make me your resting place.

Break Every Chain

He did this so that they might seek God,
and perhaps they might reach out and find him,
though he is not far from each one of us.

ACTS 17:27 CSB

There is a chance to start over—every day if we need to. From the inside out, we can be transformed and our hearts renewed. We can essentially remake ourselves with the help, healing, and transformative nature of Christ! Jesus died on the cross to promise us a life free from the bondage of sin, free from hopelessness, free from any chains that try to trap us. In Christ, we are set free. We need to hear the truth of Christ's promise for us and stop the cycle of hopelessness, defeat, and bondage to sin. All we need to do is get on our knees and pray.

You are near to me, God. In this moment, and in this room, you are so much nearer to me than I expect. I will rest in your presence, knowing that it is you who protect me. Thank you!

Ask for Wisdom

In the same way, wisdom is pleasing to you.
If you find it, you have hope for the future,
and your wishes will come true.

PROVERBS 24:14 NCV

In order to make good choices, we need to contemplate them in a godly manner and trust in the hope of our future. Many decisions affect our lives in the near future and beyond. Asking God for wisdom should be part our daily routine. In our quiet times, we can ask God to grow our love for him, to provide for and protect us, and to lead us to wise choices that honor him. Choices must be made every day. Some are very small; others are monumental. All require wisdom to assure we choose God's way for our lives.

Oh God, I pray that you would give me wisdom this day. I pray that you would place in me the fear of the Lord, so I would have a heart for wisdom. In my rising and in my resting, may I contemplate you and seek your wisdom.

Joy Complete

"Until now you have not asked for anything in my name. Ask and you will receive, and your joy will be complete."

JOHN 16:24 NIV

Jesus' followers had been with him for three years. During this time, they learned, walked out his plan, and were transformed by their relationship with the King of kings. After having their needs met by Jesus, the disciples must have been terribly anxious to think of the days ahead without him. Although they could not have understood what Jesus was saying about the Holy Spirit, they did understand that when Jesus prayed, things happened in truly astonishing ways. What joy it brings us to know that God truly loves us and cares to answer our faith-filled prayers!

Lord, may my joy in you be made complete. Help me to bring my every request to you rather than holding them all myself. Thank you for your grace and for treating me gently in all my desires and complaints.

Quiet Times

"Ask and it will be given to you;
seek and you will find;
knock and the door will be opened to you."

MATTHEW 7:7 NIV

Your quiet times might be anything but quiet. You might struggle to find solitude, and the noise might just never quit. Sometimes it feels impossible to connect with Jesus. Your time is limited, your energy is dwindling, and your attention is on a million little things. Jesus' reminder to ask, seek, and knock doesn't come with prerequisites. He doesn't say, "Ask after you've sat still for fifteen uninterrupted minutes," or "Knock only after you've memorized a psalm and listened to a worship song." Learn how to walk steadily leaning on truth, flexing your spiritual muscles as you ask, seek, and knock whenever you can.

Jesus, please teach me to come to you more readily. Help me not to hold back my complaints, my heartache, or my deepest desires. Surely you are faithful to provide.

Assurance

"This is the confidence we have in approaching God:
that if we ask anything according to his will, he hears us."

JOHN 5:14 NIV

Imagine preparing long and hard to give a presentation before a large group who had the authority to help you or squash your idea. You did your research, crafted a few witty sayings, and felt that you would receive a warm welcome. They day of your speech comes, and you walk confidently into the room. Think of your surprise when, halfway through, you start to see yawns and a few people nodding off. Discouraged, you realize that your proposal has fallen on deaf ears. When we take our concerns before the throne of grace, we are assured that God will be faithful to hear us. If our petition is within his good and perfect will, we can believe in faith that he will grant us the very thing we are asking for.

Oh Lord, you hear me in my hurt. You hear me in my pain. Please be near to me in this moment, and remind me of the confidence I have before your throne.

Astonishing

When the crowd saw this, they were filled with awe;
and they praised God, who had given such authority to man.

MATTHEW 9:7-8 NIV

God's acts are undeniably real, supernatural, and full of
incomparable power. When Jesus walked the earth, he did
an abundance of miracles, so many that the Bible couldn't
contain them all. When people gathered to see the wonders
that Jesus wrought, they were astonished and gave glory and
honor to God. They knew he was special. Some rightfully
believed that he was the Messiah, for they had never seen
anyone who spoke or moved with such authority. Since God
is the same yesterday, today, and forever, we should keep our
eyes open for his mighty wonders.

*Oh Lord, who knows the wonders you have displayed? Who
can count the stars in the sky which you have named, or the
blades of grass on this earth? I glorify you, for there is none
like you—perfect in glory.*

At a Loss

Now in the same way the Spirit also helps our weakness;
for we do not know what to pray for as we buy should,
but the Spirit Himself intercedes for us with groanings
too deep for words.

ROMANS 8:26 NASB

The Spirit is our helper in all things. There is nothing that is out of his realm of expertise. He sees it all so clearly. When we don't know how to pray, he is able to offer up intercession on our behalf. Have you ever been so grieved that all you can do is cry? Have you ever tried to formulate words to pray but found that you had nothing to offer? What then? Have you ever been surprised by sounds that escape you in desperation? God is with you in all of it. He helps us in our weakness to pray.

Holy Spirit, please move in me this day. As I try to bring my prayers before the throne, with faltering words and a lisping tongue, please give me utterance beyond human speech. Only through you can I truly speak and be understood.

At All Times

Be joyful because you have hope.
Be patient when trouble comes,
and pray at all times.

ROMANS 12:12 NCV

We cannot fabricate happy feelings, but we can become so acquainted with the hope we have in Christ that it fills us with joy even in our sorrow. When trouble comes, we know that it will not last, so we can persevere patiently. God has assured his victory in the end. Praying at all times offers the understanding that God is nearby and wants an active role in our lives. By conversing with him, living according to his Word, and taking time to listen for his voice, we can have our joy, hope, and patience renewed daily.

Lord, I am burdened and brought low by this world of woes. Be the patience within me, the joy in times of heartache. Only through you can I endure these times of difficulty. Only through you can I find the virtue to survive the trials.

Awesome God

> LORD, the God of the heavens, the great and awe-inspiring
> God who keeps his gracious covenant with those who love
> him and keep his commands.
>
> NEHEMIAH 1:5 CSB

When the Bible says that God is an awesome God, it means that he is extremely impressive. He should invoke great admiration in you. Anytime someone approaches God in the Bible, you see this. They fell on their faces. They couldn't speak. They didn't do this to put on a show; they did it because there was no other response for meeting face-to-face with the awesome, living, powerful God. In humility, on our knees before God, our posture shows that we remember who he is and who we are. He is the one true God. Let's continue in reverent worship of the one who is truly awesome.

God, you are exalted above all others! There is no god like you, and no one else deserves my praise. I live to give you glory and bring you praise. In this calling I find my truest enjoyment. May your name be lifted high this day.

Be a Blessing

Take advantage of every opportunity to be a blessing to others, especially to our brothers and sisters in the family of faith!

GALATIANS 6:10 TPT

Prayer and kindness changes people. It's not always easy to be kind to everyone, but being kind softens hearts—those of the givers and the receivers. God doesn't ask us to be kind to only those who are kind to us. He wants us to be kind to all. In fact, he commands it. He sent his Son for the whole world, and that's always reason enough to look for ways to be a blessing to others.

Holy Spirit, please open my eyes. Help me to see how I can be a blessing to others, and how I can brighten their day. May I bring your presence to others through actions of kindness and compassion.

Aware

My soul waits in hope for the LORD
More than the watchmen for the morning;
Yes, more than the watchmen for the morning.

PSALM 130:6 NASB

There is more to our world than what meets the eye. What you can see around you is the physical realm. There is also the spiritual realm. We walk around unaware of the spiritual realm, unaware of things that are happening around us. In reading the Bible, however, we see that it is very active. We know that there are evil forces, along with God and his angels. That's why we must be diligent in prayer. Just like the watchmen kept watch over the city at night, we must keep watch over our lives through prayer.

On you, Lord, do I wait. I will put all my hope in you rather than the relief I get from this world. The times are dark, but I remain unmoved in your promises. I find my consolation in the thought of your return, and I trust in your timing.

Still Before Him

"Be still, and know that I am God.
I will be exalted among the nations,
I will be exalted in the earth!"

PSALM 46:10 ESV

Stop striving. You do not fight alone. Turn to the one who is exalted to the farthest reaches of the earth and watch him work his wonders! Be still before him and take time to heed the voice of your Maker. It is he alone whom every nation will praise, and the entirety of humanity will bow before. When you face trials, rather than brazenly pushing forward or cowering in dismay, intentionally be still before God so you can witness his power and learn how you ought to walk.

Let my soul be quiet before the thought of the Almighty God. Lord, bring me to my knees in peace as I contemplate your magnificence. No nation, no earthly wonder, can stand against your holy presence. I will be still and know that you are God.

Beautiful Song

If I speak in the tongues of men or of angels, but do not have love, I am only a resounding gong or a clanging cymbal. If I have the gift of prophecy and can fathom all mysteries and all knowledge, and if I have a faith that can move mountains, but do not have love, I am nothing.

1 Corinthians 13:1-2 NIV

If you go to a concert, the orchestra, or your church, you might hear instruments in the band warming up, tuning their instruments, and practicing notes. It's a cacophony of noises and none of them fit together. It's painful to the ears! But if you wait long enough, the music begins. When all the instruments play in harmony, it's beautiful. You have many talents and spiritual gifts, but if you aren't acting in love, you sound like those instruments warming up. Don't rely on your talents. Put your trust in Jesus and submit your gifts to him. When you use your gifts in humble love, suddenly it becomes music.

What am I if I do not love, Lord? Give me purpose by living for others rather than myself. May I love just as you have loved me. Be my inspiration. I want to become more like you, sharing your love for others through the gifts you have given me.

Wonderfully Sovereign

Yours, LORD, is the greatness and the power and the glory
and the majesty and the splendor, for everything in heaven
and earth is yours.

1 CHRONICLES 29:11 NIV

It is good to have a king who is totally good and totally in
control. If anyone should receive recognition for anything, it
should be our God who has shown himself perfect in every
way. No one else is fit to accept such praise. God stands
wonderfully sovereign over all things. He deserves praise for
all "the greatness and the power and the glory." Let us rejoice
that we have a God worth praising, since he is the mighty
Creator of all things and the gentle Redeemer of our souls.

*Who has authored anything besides you, Lord? This world,
with all its splendors and glories, is yours. Heaven, in all its
infinite perfection is yours. Truly every creative thought is
yours.*

Beauty

He has made everything beautiful in its time.
He has also set eternity in the human heart;
yet no one can fathom what God has done
from beginning to end.

ECCLESIASTES 3:11 NIV

Beauty is captivating. We can see, hear, taste, and feel it. Think of magnificent mountains with water cascading down jagged cliffs and through green canopies. Or imagine the sound in an orchestra hall, exquisite music pulling you through the story of song. What about the taste of an amazing meal: spices and seasonings creating a salivation celebration. The beauty of touch exists as well: gripping the new leather on a steering wheel, running fingers along the smoothness of purified metal, and refreshingly cold water splashing against your skin on a hot day. Many things around us are beautiful, and we only need to pause a moment to experience them and remember that God has created it all. He is to be thanked for the beauty in our lives.

Beautiful Lord, I am captivated by the love you show through your created world. There is nothing good apart from you. I will honor you because there is nothing glorious apart from you.

Because He Is God

Give unto the LORD the glory due to His name;
Worship the LORD in the beauty of holiness.

PSALM 29:2 NKJV

There are at least a million reasons to worship God, and each day he adds to them by forgiving us, blessing us, and dazzling us with his power, glory, and beauty. No matter how much we write down, recall, or read about, we can never come close to identifying all the reasons he is worthy of our praise. So let's give it him. Because he's God and because he's holy, give him the glory he deserves.

Lord, be glorified this day. I pray that a thousand voices at once, from every station in life and every nation, would give you praise every minute. May your heart be seen in how we treat each other. Help me to give you glory through more than just my words.

Being an Encouragement

May our Lord Jesus Christ himself and God our Father...
encourage your hearts and strengthen you in
every good deed and word.

2 THESSALONIANS 2:16–17 NIV

We all need encouragement. Sometimes it comes from unlikely sources like complete strangers, and sometimes it comes from those we love. Either way, encouragement has an incredible impact on our lives. Receiving encouragement is great, but being an encourager is scriptural. Imagine when we whisper praise to God. Imagine how he feels when we shout our thanksgiving to him. God serves us in outstanding ways, and he deserves our daily praise, love, and attention.

I am weak, Lord. I cannot do any good on my own or resist any temptation. Please equip me to do every good work, so I am not a slave to evil but rather to righteousness.

Being Heard

Hear the sound of my prayer,
when I cry out to you for help.
I raise my hands toward your Most Holy Place.

PSALM 28:2 NCV

Surrender your cares to Jesus every day. Let him lift the
weight of your heavy burdens and flood you with peace.
His love is the sustaining force of your life, and that will
never change. Trust him to work miracles of mercy in every
impossible situation you face. You are not alone. He is with
you and for you. Cry out for his help whenever you need it.
He is watching and waiting.

*God, how long can I go on my own? I need you, and I need
you to hear me. I need to know you are near me, and I need
to know that I am more than the failures of my past. Please,
God, hear me.*

Believe in Faith

Without faith it is impossible to please God, because anyone who comes to him must believe that he exists and that he rewards those who earnestly seek him.

HEBREWS 11:6 NIV

To truly follow God is not simply to uphold our end of an agreement. We are not bound to obedience out of some obligation or threat. Real faith overflows into our behavior and it becomes a joy to follow our Lord. The only place we want to be is with him because we love him. If faith is not part of our lives, no amount of moral dealings will please God. He is looking for an active and loving relationship with us, not a robotic and reluctant religious adherence.

Lord, please give me real faith. May it not be a faith of my family or of my community alone, but a faith of my own. May I own it, deep inside of me, and may it affect who I am as a person.

Better Balance

Grow in the grace and knowledge of our Lord and Savior
Jesus Christ. To him be the glory, both now
and to the day of eternity. Amen.

2 PETER 3:18 NIV

Some days it feels like we're on a merry-go-round that
keeps going faster and faster. We're bogged down with
heavy responsibilities, and we scramble to get everything
done, usually without success. Sound familiar? That stress
can take a toll on our time spent with God. Overwhelming
moments are a good reminder to sit down and take stock
of how we can get our lives in better balance. Nobody can
do everything and do it all well, but one thing must be a
priority—spending time with God.

*Lord, plant me deep in your grace and knowledge. Make
them the foundation of my actions and help me to be faithful
in pursuing them. How can I give you glory, if your grace
and knowledge are far from me?*

March

We are confident that he hears us whenever we ask for anything that pleases him.

1 John 5:14 nlt

Most Important

My lips will glorify you
because your faithful love is better than life.
So I will bless you as long as I live;
at your name, I will lift up my hands.

PSALM 63:3-4 CSB

We tend to cling pretty hard to the stuff in our lives—our home, our clothes, our shoes, our electronics, our music. Even our friends, our home, and family can seem to be the most important things of all. And yet, the Bible tells us that God's love is better than life. That love is better than anything or anyone we have or know. When you spend time with God, you become even more aware of his amazing love. Everything else pales in comparison. The more you know how much God loves you, the more you'll find that trusting and praising him comes naturally.

Oh Lord, there is none like you. My life exists for your glory, so I will lift up my hands and praise your name with all that is inside of me. May you be exalted in my heart and in this world.

Better than Sleep

My mouth will praise you with joyful lips,
when I remember you upon my bed,
and meditate on you in the watches of the night.

PSALM 63:5-6 ESV

What can possibly feel better after a day of hard work than the invitation of a soft bed? What could be more inviting than sinking a weary head into the pillow? Or offer sweet soul satisfaction like a quiet house asleep? Unless of course it's neither asleep nor quiet. The Psalmist must have had sleepless nights too. But he found a higher purpose even more satisfying than sleep. His nighttime satisfaction came from remembering God while he lay on his bed. He praised God in the watches of the night, and through those long, lonely hours. Intentional praise during nights when sleep doesn't come is a wonderful way to remove cares and tension.

Lord, in my resting and in my waking, may my thoughts rise to you. Be the meditation of my heart with my thoughts on you in every moment.

Best Friend

My heart has heard you say,
"Come and talk with me."
And my heart responds,
"Lord, I am coming."

Psalm 27:8 NLT

When you have a best friend, there's no end to the time you want to spend with them. Maybe you and your bestie talk over multiple platforms on social media, through texting, and in real life, all at the same time. There's something about that friendship that never gets old. You know they want to hear from you, and you feel the same. Jesus is the best friend you will ever find. He wants to hear from you too. He cares deeply about you and everything that happens in your life. He asks you to spend time with him and listen to him speak, yet he also wants to listen to you. Won't you share your life with him today?

Jesus, why do I withhold my heart from you? Why do I ever hesitate to speak to you? I run to you this day. I give myself to you. Please give me your intimate presence.

Seen Later

> "Whoever makes himself great will be made humble. Whoever makes himself humble will be made great."
>
> MATTHEW 23:12 NCV

Like a stagehand who, thinking they are alone, bursts into flawless, glorious song only to learn the director was sitting in the darkened seats, your hidden gifts will be recognized. Like an anonymous donor whose identity is finally discovered, your silent contributions will be celebrated. Just as those who seek recognition will one day receive the gift of humility, so too will those who keep themselves low receive the gift of recognition.

Lord, may I live not for my own glory but for yours. I was made for your glory, so why should I pursue my own just to be met with disappointment and loneliness. Thank you for calling me your own.

In Admiration

What, after all, is Apollos? And what is Paul? Only servants, through whom you came to believe—as the Lord has assigned to each his task. I planted the seed, Apollos watered it, but God has been making it grow. So neither the one who plants nor the one who waters is anything, but only God, who makes things grow. The one who plants and the one who waters have one purpose, and they will each be rewarded according to their own labor.

1 Corinthians 3:5-8 niv

It is good to have mentors and those you look up to. It is good for you to be encouraged by the lives of other believers. You might have a favorite author, social media influencer, or pastor. There isn't anything inherently wrong with that. In your admiration, it is paramount that you ascribe glory where it is due. God is the one who is truly at work. If your worship of another person has surpassed your worship for God, then you need to rearrange your focus.

God, help me today to see the proper place of honor I should give to those around me in the faith. May I remember that it is you who does the work, not just in me, but in everyone I look up to.

Boast in God

The one who boasts should boast in this:
that he understands and knows me—
that I am the LORD, showing faithful love,
justice, and righteousness on the earth,
for I delight in these things.
This is the LORD's declaration.

JEREMIAH 9:24 CSB

All of our accomplishments amount to nothing if they are not for the sake of Christ. Everything apart from God will one day pass away. So, the greatest boasting we should do is in what God has done for us. We ought to boast that we know God, for that is something to be greatly desired. When we are transparent about our life in Christ, others may want what we have found.

God of all justice, may I give to you the respect you have merited. Truly it is you and you alone who deal justly with all. I have no complaint against you because you are above them all.

Bold Prayers

"Whatever you ask in my name, this I will do,
that the Father may be glorified in the Son."

JOHN 14:13 ESV

Directly before this statement, Jesus told his disciples that
they would do all that he did in his ministry and more. This
is no small statement! He was speaking of miracles, signs,
and wonders: large displays of God's power. We were never
meant to stay small in prayer or in faith. When he said to ask
anything, he meant it. This includes the big, bold prayers that
would be impossible to accomplish in our humanity. May
we take Jesus at his word today and ask him for the greater
things. He has not stopped moving in power, so let's not stop
asking him to show up in wonderful ways.

*How can I be bolder today, Jesus? How can I walk in the
confidence with which you walked? May I mimic the courage
of the gospel, showing to others its power through my trust
in it.*

Make Your Request

If we know that he hears us—whatever we ask—
we know that we have what we asked of him.

1 JOHN 5:15 NIV

God loves his children. He wants us to be happy, to feel fulfilled. When we approach him with our wants and needs, he truly hears us. The next time you feel as if your requests are too unimportant to bother God about, remind yourself that he is always listening. Though he may not answer you in the way you expect, he is right there beside you ready to lend an ear.

God, you hear me. You listen to me, and you are not prone to coming up short. Give me trust in your plan today, so I do not despair.

Bones

With every bone in my body I will praise him:
"Lord, who can compare with you?
Who else rescues the helpless from the strong?
Who else protects the helpless and poor
from those who rob them?"

Psalm 35:10 NLT

In times where we are grieved by injustice, we need to go to the one and only just King. It can be confusing to know when and how God intervenes and protects because we still experience darkness in our world and there are many who are helpless and poor. God is working in our world and if you pay attention, you will notice the ways that he is using others to look out for those in need. He is a good God and there is no one like him, so praise him with every bone in your body!

God in heaven, how great you are! May the very marrow in my bones exult in your glory, raising you above every name. I live to praise your name, showing your glory to the nations with every brother and sister.

Both Necessary

After He had sent the crowds away,
He went up on the mountain by Himself to pray;
and when it was evening, He was there alone.

MATTHEW 14:23 NASB

It would be easy to stop our consideration of Jesus' alone time here, recognizing the example of balance he set by healing then restoring, teaching then retreating. It's a wonderful lesson, but also an incomplete one. Jesus didn't retreat to find a hot spring and get in touch with himself. As nice as that sounds, and as pleasant as a good soak can be, Jesus went off by himself to pray. He knew that alone is never really alone. The Holy Spirit is always with us, connecting, rejuvenating, and replenishing our stores of patience and peace. Let us not waste our alone time being alone! Rather, let us draw on the intimacy with our Lord that is only possible when we are alone with him.

God, may I not fall out of balance. May I learn to know when to be still in your presence and when to live deeply in community.

Bottled Up

As I stood there in silence—
not even speaking of good things—
the turmoil within me grew worse.

PSALM 39:2 NLT

The Psalmist here is describing one of those moments where
you bottle up all of your emotions. Can you relate to those
times where you are feeling so much turmoil on the inside,
but you just can't find the words to express yourself? You
might overanalyze how to say accurately what you feel,
worried that it will come out in the wrong way. Maybe you are
concerned about how the people who hear you will react. The
trouble is, turmoil grows when you can't let it out. Direct your
emotions toward Jesus. He will listen, and he will help you.

*God, I just need to let loose today. I need to level upon
you all of the vitriol and harsh thoughts raging within me.
Remind me you are faithful and will not leave me because of
my difficult emotions.*

Breakthrough

I set my face toward the LORD God to make request by prayer and supplications, with fasting, sackcloth, and ashes.

DANIEL 9:3 NKJV

Are you waiting for a breakthrough in your circumstances? Maybe you have been praying for an unbelieving family member, a strained relationship, an answer to your financial stress, or clarity for a big decision ahead. Fasting doesn't often top the list of what to do when you really need that breakthrough, and it's not that hard to guess why it isn't a popular option. Eating is one of the most necessary and natural impulses; it takes a lot of self-control and personal effort to stop. Consider what the Bible says about fasting and notice how it goes hand in hand with prayer. There is a certain humility that accompanies fasting; it requires sobriety of heart, reflection, and focus. It shows a different level of commitment to whatever you are praying for.

God, my heart is set toward you. I need you, and I desire your plan to be made known to me. Please notice the supplication of my heart, and do not turn away from me.

Breathtaking

How could I be silent when it's time to praise you?
Now my heart sings out, bursting with joy—
a bliss inside that keeps me singing,
"I can never thank you enough!"

PSALM 30:12 TPT

God's creation is astounding. To truly be stunned means it is hard to put into words what you are seeing. When we are taken aback by something God made, when we truly grasp that he made it and made it so well, we should be full of praise. We don't applaud the creation; our exultation should arise to the Creator. He is the one deserving of the worship. If anything, whatever takes our breath away should end in glory to the one who made it.

Sweet Jesus, the joy in my heart is like a horse running free. I am fearfully and wonderfully in awe of all you have done and all you are, so I turn to you in praise. May you be honored on this day.

Bring Everything

Is anyone among you in trouble?
Let them pray.
Is anyone happy?
Let them sing songs of praise.

JAMES 5:13 NIV

Are you satisfied with your prayer life? How much time do you spend talking to the Lord? Whether you ask for help the moment you need it or keep a list of things to pray about when you can really focus on it, Jesus loves to hear from you. It it's a quick thank you upon receiving a blessing, or a more thoughtful recitation of all the day's glories at the end of it, he is delighted to receive your gratitude. As many ways as there are to converse, there are ways to pray. Jesus is waiting for you to draw close to him.

Dear God, please work in my heart to produce a habit of prayer and praise. May I learn to give my time to you rather than whittling it away with idle pastimes.

Bubbling Over

We laughed and laughed, and overflowed with gladness.
We were left shouting for joy and singing your praise.
All the nations saw it and joined in, saying,
"The Lord has done great miracles for them!"

PSALM 126:2 TPT

Laughter is one of the greatest sounds in the world. An old married couple dancing. A toddler being tickled. A pair of best friends sharing a joke. When you hear laughter, you can't help but crack a smile yourself. Imagine what God must feel when he hears his children laughing, singing, and praising him together. Imagine what happiness must sound like to him. Picture a room full of believers singing in harmony to show their love for him. What a joyous, beautiful sound that must be!

Holy Spirit, is there anything to compare to your joy? Is there anything I can say or write to capture the gladness you have put in my heart? Dwell in me today, perfecting the good work you have started.

Burdens

Bear one another's burdens,
and thereby fulfill the law of Christ.

GALATIANS 6:2 NASB

Will you pray for me? Does this sound like something you would say? If it doesn't, the Lord wants you to know that it should. We aren't meant to carry our troubles on our own. He loves our sincere prayers for help, and he hears us. How much louder are those cries for help when echoed by the voices of our friends and families? There are also times our needs extend beyond prayer. Sometimes we need help. When we need it, the Father encourages us to ask for it. As we are all one with Christ, he longs for us to be one with each other by bearing one another's burdens and sharing in his love.

Lord, teach me in humility to walk alongside other people. Teach me to lift them up, rather than walking past them and their issues. May I make their burdens my own and be an uplifting source to them.

Life and Healing

For you who revere my name,
the sun of righteousness will rise with healing in its rays.

MALACHI 4:2 NIV

Spring is a time of rejoicing: the new flowers, the melting snow, the gradual increase of daylight and warmth. Isn't it great that Easter falls into this season? The work Jesus did on the cross causes great rejoicing. Jesus has risen from the dead; the sun of righteousness has risen with healing in his wings! This is a great reason for us to celebrate! Just like we bask in the newness and wonder of spring, let the resurrection of Christ bring joy to your heart.

God, you have made all things new through the resurrection of your Son. Please bring the sun of righteousness to shine over this day, giving glory to you and sustaining me by its rays.

Time for Singing

The flowers appear on the earth,
the time of singing has come,
and the voice of the turtledove is heard in our land.

SONG OF SOLOMON 2:12 ESV

Sometimes, the seasons of our lives do not align with the seasons of the earth. Though we may be in the dead of winter, perhaps our relationships and hope are thriving like the fruit of summer. Maybe we find ourselves in a time of letting go, like autumn, but a friend is experiencing the renewal of spring, where new life is popping up. When the time of singing comes, it is a joy to share it with loved ones. Our shared gladness and celebration are as meaningful as our shared suffering and grief. Let's not shrink back from times of rejoicing with those we love for the new life that breaks through after the barrenness of winter. When flowers bloom, let's enjoy their scent and beauty.

It is a time of rejoicing, Lord! It is a time for me to sing your praise, echoing the good works you have done from the creation of the universe up to now. Let me be a trumpet of your testimony.

Call Upon Him

Oh, give thanks to the LORD!
Call upon His name;
Make known His deeds among the peoples!

1 CHRONICLES 16:8 NKJV

In this moment, you have an opportunity. Every moment, every breath, is a chance to call upon the Lord. Raise your awareness and turn your attention to him. With a whispered prayer or a shout for help, call upon him. He is always near. He is always full of strength and power to help you. Has God turned ashes into beauty in your life? Share your story with someone who needs a boost of hope. Has he provided in unexpected ways? Thank him. When you recognize his incredible mercy, be encouraged and share it, so faith may be increased and courage bolstered.

Dear Jesus, there is such an abundance of reasons to give thanks. There is an overwhelming number of ways for me to praise you and shout your testimony! May I explore them anew today.

A Loving Mother

"How could a loving mother forget her nursing child and not deeply love the one she bore? Even if a there is a mother who forgets her child, I could never, no never, forget you."

ISAIAH 49:15 TPT

Do you sometimes get so busy that you forget about the people around you? Mothers might be forgetful at times, but they don't usually forget their children. On the rare occasion they do, God reminds you that he never forgets. He is the perfect parent who will always look out for your needs. Some of us have family who are reliable, and others might not. Take some time to pray for your mother, or a mother figure, and your relationship with her.

God, thank you for being so loving and faithful to me. Thank you for offering your time and attention without reserve! May I learn to appreciate those in my life who have acted the same way as you have toward me.

Calling God

"Ask me and I will tell you remarkable secrets
you do not know about things to come."

JEREMIAH 33:3 NLT

In order to live a happy life, prayer needs to be a priority
for us. Here are a few tips to help you call out to God. First,
make it a habit. Just like any other healthy habit, if you miss
a day or forget, start again, and again, until it becomes a
habitual part of your life. Second, keep a record of your
requests and things prayed about. It's so encouraging when
you can look back and see God answering your prayers.
Third, pray out loud when you can. Verbalizing your prayers
can help you focus. Lastly, learn to pray often—when your
mind wanders to a specific person, when you are met with
frustration, even when you are doing dishes. These are all
opportunities to call out to God.

*God, why do I hesitate to call on you? Why do I ever try to
fix my own problems, when it never, ever turns out? I pray
that I would grow in dependence on you, taking my every
care and need to your throne.*

Calming

Casting all your cares on him,
because he cares about you.
1 PETER 5:7 CSB

Have you ever been told not to worry? To just relax and
let everything work out? Sounds easy, and over-simplified,
doesn't it? God never intended for us to suffer in anguish
over uncertainty. From the beginning, he designed us to
depend on him for everything, including our next breath.
He has proven his faithfulness. We can ask him to take the
reins, provide what we need, and thank him for his constant
protection and provision.

*God, in my anguish please be my calm. Be the reason I can
last another day, another hour, another second. Without
you carrying my cares, I will stumble. Please help me today
because no one else will.*

Caring for Others

Let each of you look out not only for his own interests,
but also for the interests of others.

PHILIPPIANS 2:4 NKJV

When we pray, how much of it is consumed with requests
for protection and blessing for ourselves? Do we take time
to simply praise God for who he is and what he has done?
Do we beseech him on behalf of others? When someone else
has a problem, are we quick to help in their time of need?
Do we care for others the same way we care for ourselves,
remembering that we are all parts of the same body? It is not
God's intention that we care only for ourselves and stay at a
safe distance from the mess of life and others' problems. If
we love God, we will care for his people.

*Why is it, God, that I find my own needs so much more
pressing than the needs of those around me? I continually
focus on myself even though it often leads to stumbling. Give
me eyes for the interests of those around me, so I would not
forget them.*

Not a Fad

They celebrate your abundant goodness
and joyfully sing of your righteousness.

PSALM 145:7 NIV

God is not a hype or a fad. He is not a popular celebrity who will fade from our memories in time, unable to hold the interest of our children, and unheard of by our children's children. God's name has been proclaimed on the earth throughout every generation, and it always will be. God's people, old and young, rejoice because of who God is and what he's done. This spans all ages across the globe. We can celebrate God on our own, in our hearts, declaring his righteousness and singing his praises.

In the privacy of my room, when no one is watching, may I still be praising you, Lord! Give me perseverance in praise, continuing in my worship as long as your blessings do not cease.

Appreciating Friends

I come to your altar, O LORD,
singing a song of thanksgiving
and telling of all your wonders.

PSALM 26:6-7 NLT

When was the last time we truly took the time to thank our closest people for their friendship? The ones who have seen us through the long nights and even longer mornings. The ones who celebrate our smallest wins and show up to cheer us on as we run races. Just as we sing songs of thanksgiving to the Lord who does wonderful things, let's not neglect the importance of singing the praise of our faithful friends. God is not offended when we celebrate the people in our lives. He takes joy in our jubilation! He is a delight-filled God who loves it when we show love to others.

God, please teach me to celebrate my friends. Help me to give praise for them as I should, focusing on their strengths and victories rather than their weaknesses and flaws.

Celebrated

Celebrate with praises the God and Father of our Lord Jesus Christ, who has shown us his extravagant mercy. For his fountain of mercy has given us a new life—we are reborn to experience a living, energetic hope through the resurrection of Jesus Christ from the dead.

1 PETER 1:3 TPT

Life is worth celebrating. It is precious. The things we value are things we celebrate. March is the month we celebrate the beginning of spring in the northern hemisphere. It is a time of new life, beginnings, and fresh creativity. In these seasons it feels good to be alive especially if you have been locked away by a frigid winter. Whether the start of spring, a new life, or the end of a cold winter, when we celebrate, it is done best with others. That is the greatest way to enjoy what has occurred. It reminds us of our created purpose to enjoy all that God has blessed us with.

Father, who is there like you? You have raised me with your Son, so I might be presented to you blameless on the final judgment day. I thank you this day, for all that you have done and promise to do.

Changes

My enemy has chased me.
He has knocked me to the ground and forces me
to live in darkness like those in the grave.

PSALM 143:3 NLT

It's not the happiest verse in Scriptures, but it tells a story that many of us experience. Have you felt this way before? Do you feel this way right now? It's normal and right to express the way someone or some experience has made you feel. God is listening to you right now, so why not share your concerns and heartaches. It is sometimes in the expression of despair where we are able to release and let go of the darkness.

God, why am I here? There is so much pain in this place I am in, yet my situation does not change. Give me faith in your plan when I cannot see it. I am surrounded by reasons to give up, but I continue to trust in you.

Chaos Climates

I heard a loud shout from the throne, saying, "Look, God's home is now among his people! He will live with them, and they will be his people. God himself will be with them. He will wipe every tear from their eyes, and there will be no more death or sorrow or crying or pain. All these things are gone forever."

REVELATION 21:3-4 NLT

Prior to Christ's sacrifice, sin separated people from God. Atonement had to be made for sins in the form of animal sacrifices, and people had to travel to the temple for their prayers and offerings. When Jesus came to fulfil the law and offer himself as the final and ultimate sacrifice, he explained that it was no longer necessary to travel to the temple to worship God. We have been given direct access to God through prayer. This is an astounding privilege. One day when we are called home, we will have an even more personal and intimate relationship with our Creator. All death and sorrow will be gone, and we will walk with God just like he intended from the beginning.

Lord, what a glorious day it will be when all evil is washed away like dross! Teach me to eagerly await the day of your revelation. The whole earth is groaning in anticipation of your reconciliation.

Optimism

Rejoice always, pray without ceasing,
give thanks in all circumstances;
for this is the will of God in Christ Jesus for you.

1 Thessalonians 5:16-18 esv

If only all the commandments were this easy: rejoice, pray, and give thanks. This sounds so achievable until you add in the qualifiers. Rejoice always? Pray without ceasing? Give thanks in all circumstances? This actually sounds hard. Is it even possible? How do we rejoice when our hearts are broken, remember to pray when we're watching TV, or give thanks for lost jobs, broken appliances, or troubles with family? For every heartbreak, God wants to be our healer. Before we relax, he wants us to check in. For every disappointment, he wants to be the restorer of our hope.

Give me optimism, Jesus, because the situations of this life do not offer me a reason. You are my only source of hope in a barren landscape, so I lean into you and your promises of eternity.

Choose Wisely

This world is fading away,
along with everything that people crave.
But anyone who does what pleases God will live forever.

1 JOHN 2:17 NLT

We can use busyness as an ally in our quest to do great things for God. When we do, it's very easy to miss out on God himself. Sometimes even good things get in the way of eternal things. When we fill our schedule with endless acts of service, committees, and activities, we neglect God in the busyness. Suddenly, we become more his employees and less his children. God wants a relationship with us: to just sit with us. And that's enough. We can pray and get to know him more through his Word.

The choice between evil and good is the choice between life and death, Lord. Help me to see the unsure footing of my unsaved contemporaries and recognize how blessed I am to be called your child.

No Matter What

I will glory in the LORD;
let the afflicted hear and rejoice.
Glorify the LORD with me;
let us exalt his name together.

PSALM 34:2-3 NIV

Do we only praise God for something after he has given it, or do we praise him ahead of time in faith, knowing that he will always be good no matter what happens? We should look at difficulties in life as miracles waiting to happen, as chances for God to show his goodness and bring us closer to his heart. Can you choose to praise him today in spite of your circumstances?

God, make me a reason for the afflicted to praise your name! Make me a reason for the afflicted to have hope and to remember that you act. I am made perfect through worshiping you, so I will continue to lift up my praises.

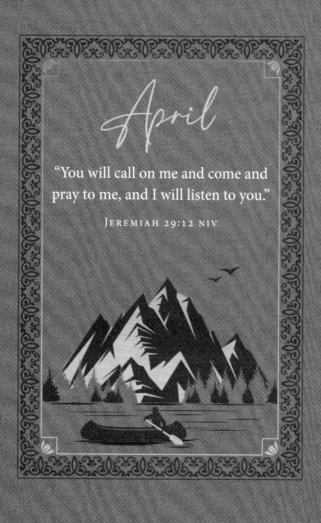

April

"You will call on me and come and pray to me, and I will listen to you."

JEREMIAH 29:12 NIV

Chosen by God

You are not like that, for you are a chosen people. You are royal priests, a holy nation, God's very own possession. As a result, you can show others the goodness of God, for he called you out of the darkness into his wonderful light.

1 PETER 2:9 NLT

One important way our lives would be different if we lived as chosen ones is that we would praise God more. When you have good news, it can be almost impossible to keep it to yourself. Good news is meant to be shared. We have the good news that we are chosen by God, plus the even better news that this is not an exclusive club. When you proclaim his goodness in your life, be sure to tell others that they too are loved by God, that he wants to welcome them into his family and know them fully.

If I am chosen, God, then how am I acting differently? Please help me to see the difference between my life and the life of someone who doesn't have a relationship with you. If there is no difference, put me on the right path.

Clay

O LORD, you are our Father;
we are the clay, and you are our potter;
we are all the work of your hand

ISAIAH 64:8 ESV

Life can be busy. Whatever season you are in, there are always things to be done. More often than not, our wellbeing is cast aside because other things need to be tended to. Our Creator says that we are jars of clay. If left out and not tended to, that jar can dry out and crack. If we give God our obedience and our time, he promises us his abundance and peace, quenching our very driest parts. We receive his renewal when we sit in his presence, letting him fill our spirits with his love and gentle, encouraging words.

Shape me and mold me, God. Take my form and craft it into your image, so I would give greater glory to you. Without you, I am nothing, so please dwell in me and make me your image bearer.

On the Surface

"You clean the outside of the cup and dish, but inside they are full of greed and self-indulgence. You are like whitewashed tombs, which look beautiful on the outside but on the inside are full of the bones of the dead and everything unclean."

MATTHEW 23:25, 27 NIV

Is your room a mess? If it's pretty clean, check the closet and under the bed. Chances are you'll find a pile or two. Or worse. It takes a great deal of patience and perseverance to really deal with a mess instead of moving it out of sight. This can be translated into our emotional, mental, and spiritual lives as well. Do we present a together, happy, organized face to the world while our hearts overflow with clutter, pressure, and disarray?

God, I cannot tolerate my hypocrisy anymore. Without you, I cannot make a change in me. I can only change my appearance and fool the world. Please change me from within so I might be pleasing to you.

Clear Views

Don't turn your face away from me.
You're the God of my salvation;
how can you reject your servant in anger?
You've been my only hope,
so don't forsake me now when I need you!

PSALM 27:9 TPT

Perceptions of God verses who God really is can throw us off track. We collect ideas about God or who we want him to be from our experiences, relationships, and interactions with the church or its members. Sometimes we try to fit God into a box of our own making, labeling him in a certain fashion. This is all harmful to our view of God. It's so important to read your Bible to find out who God truly is, and how he responds toward you. The Bible, accompanied by honest prayer, can bring so much clarity; it's like turning on the defrost function when your windscreen is foggy.

Dear Lord, please bless me with your presence today. Let your face shine upon me, and do not let me be alone in my struggles! I need you, and I do not know how to manage without you.

Comfort in Stress

May the God of hope fill you with all joy and peace as you
trust in him, so that you may overflow with hope by the
power of the Holy Spirit.

ROMANS 15:13 NIV

The biggest fights with people we love often come during
times of greatest stress: buying a home, starting a new job,
studying for finals, or dealing with health problems, to name
a few. Sometimes, we're so consumed with our circumstances
that we forget God. Instead of going to him for peace and
comfort, we look to others to fill that need. If our friends or
family are also overwhelmed, there might be nothing left to
give. Next time life is more than you can handle, go to God.
He is always enough.

*Jesus, who do I have to comfort me but you? You are my
faithful friend, always there for me in times of need or
trouble. Please fill me with all joy and peace as I trust in you
this day.*

Spilling Over

I spill out my heart to you
and tell you all my troubles.

PSALM 142:2 TPT

Whatever is in your heart today, spill it out to the Lord. Tell him your worries and your troubles. Don't hold anything back. He cares for you. When you are desperate, overwhelmed, and about to give up, look to the Lord for help, and he will show you the way to go. The Lord is your hiding place, and he will not abandon you. Cry out to him in your distress and pour out your praises in your celebration. Wherever you are, whatever you are facing, bring it all before the Lord.

God, life is filled to the brim with experiences of beauty and pain. I cannot fathom the depth of your love, but I pray it would be made real to me in this place of difficulty as I struggle to believe and have faith.

Confident Prayer

The prayer of faith will save the sick, and the Lord will raise him up. And if he has committed sins, he will be forgiven.

JAMES 5:15 NKJV

God has a plan for our prayer lives. Yes, he already knows what will happen in the future, but he has also planned for our prayers to instigate events that are to come. The Bible tells us that the prayer of a righteous person has great power. That means believers who have been made righteous by Jesus' sacrifice have the power to speak healing and light into people's lives if it is God's will.

Lord Jesus, please make me a man of healing. Help me to speak life and refreshment into people's lives, so they would believe in you and in your ability to heal all wounds. I pray today over those in my life who are suffering.

Considering the Creator

When I consider Your heavens, the work of Your fingers,
the moon and the stars, which you have ordained,
what is man that You are mindful of him,
and the son of man that You visit him?

PSALM 8:3-4 NKJV

We experience such exhilaration while exploring the wonders of nature, yet often disregard the Creator from whose imagination every natural wonder originated. We fail to give him credit and forsake any exploratory notions of realizing him. The mountains and the oceans were his idea, as were the clouds and the stars. Mesmerized humans will even misdirect worship toward the heavens, falling short of the one who rules them from his heavenly throne. Far more brilliant, majestic, and exciting than any of the wonders we have witnessed in the world is he who fashioned them all.

God, I am nothing worthy of your consideration, yet you have chosen to set me by your side. You are the only thing worthy of my consideration, yet I continually forget you. Today I marvel in your majesty.

Consistent Effort

"Everyone who asks will receive.
The one who searches will find.
And everyone who knocks will have the door opened."

LUKE 11:10 NCV

No matter how comfortable or desperate you feel today, look to the Lord. He meets you with the abundance of his marvelous mercy no matter what state you are in. He is with you even now. Ask him for what you need. Search him out and you will find him. He is closer than you realize. Knock on heaven's door, and he will open it for you. You do not have to pray perfectly, do things just right, or pretend to be what you are not. Jesus covers you with his overwhelmingly perfect love. Do not give up today.

Jesus, I will continue to bring my prayers before you. Please answer them. I will not cease to wrestle with you over the trials I am facing because only through you can I find the answers I need.

Constant Praise

From the rising of the sun to its going down
The LORD's name is to be praised.

PSALM 113:3 NKJV

What would it look like to be someone who praises God from the time you awaken each morning until the time you fall asleep each night? Not only would you be pleasing God as you worship him constantly, but you would also affect an incredible change in your personal outlook. Intentional, continual praise results in real, lasting joy. When you choose to look at each moment as a moment in which to be thankful, then you will find beauty, joy, and satisfaction.

Is there ever a moment, Lord God, where I could not be in awe of you? Your glory and your wonders are without boundaries. This day, please open my eyes to the glory all around me, so my heart would be in a mindset of praise.

Contagious Kindness

I will tell of the kindnesses of the LORD,
the deeds for which he is to be praised,
according to all the LORD has done for us…
according to his compassion and many kindnesses.

ISAIAH 63:7 NIV

Early in life, many of us learned that Jesus loves us. We have learned that he is mighty and that his righteousness requires our own. But what happens when we recognize his kindness? It is in the moment we realize that Jesus has stepped into our personal situation that our spirits quicken in love and gratitude toward him. A new understanding of his omnipotence is born; it makes us want to shout and sing! Our Father in heaven, who loves us, joyfully accepts this praise. He shows himself in the tender compassion of his response to our needs and desires.

Merciful Lord Jesus, I praise you for the endless blessings you have bestowed upon me and the people around me. I praise you because there is nothing in comparison to all that you have created, redeemed, and loved!

Continued Devotion

They were continually devoting themselves to the apostles'
teaching and to fellowship, to the breaking of bread
and to prayer.

ACTS 2:42 NASB

Spanning time and crossing cultures, the church has taken
many different forms and faces. But the original functions
of the Church remain the same. Christians are to devote
themselves to learning more about the Lord Jesus and his
Word just as they always have. We are called to fellowship
with one another—to offer strength and encouragement to
the body of believers. Similar to how the early Christians
broke bread together and shared whatever they had with one
another, we are expected to use what we have to help meet
the needs of our brothers and sisters in Christ.

*What am I spending my time on? Is my life a story of
devotion and love, or is it a story of my own agenda? Make
my life a prayer to you, Lord, so I wouldn't be found wasting
away my precious time in this life.*

Perpetual Praise

I will praise the LORD at all times;
his praise is always on my lips

PSALM 34:1 NCV

It's relatively easy to sing God's praises when all is going well in our lives: when he blesses us with something we asked for, when he heals us, or when he directly answers a prayer. We naturally turn and give him praise and glory for good things. What about when things aren't going well? What about in dry times, painful times, or times of waiting? Do we only praise God for something after he's given it, or do we praise him ahead of time in faith, knowing that he will always be good no matter what happens? We should look at all difficulties in life as miracles waiting to happen—chances for God to show his goodness and bring us closer to his heart.

Who am I, Lord, that you would love me? Who am I, that you would bless me with your presence? What bounty I have found, beyond all measure and estimation: this love that I have in you! I am your child, and you are my God.

Continuous Faith

I've written this letter to you who believe in the name of the Son of God so that you will be assured and know without a doubt that you have eternal life.

1 JOHN 5:13 TPT

When you first believe in Jesus, there is an excitement and a newness about it that inspires you. But as the years go by, doubts can grow and continuing to live in a godless world can take its toll. You may start to wonder about the faith you found. It's important to be in God's Word, praying to find encouragement and perseverance. It's also important to have spiritual mentors in the faith who can help you when times get tough. If you don't have anyone, pray about who you could ask to partner with you in faith.

God, please give me the assurance I need this day. Whether it is through a mentor, through a friend, or through your Word, please remind me of the truth that I am irrevocably yours. Nothing can separate me from the redemption I have in you.

Counted as Righteous

He brought him outside and said, "Look toward heaven, and number the stars, if you are able to number them." Then he said to him, "So shall your offspring be." And he believed the LORD, and he counted it to him as righteousness.

GENESIS 15:5-6 ESV

What are you praying for that you feel God has not given you yet? The story of God's promise to Abram and Sarah reminds us that it isn't about what we say or do that saves us; rather, it is what we believe. Abram and Sarah would have undoubtedly felt skeptical that God would give them as many descendants as the stars in the sky as they wrestled with having even one child in their old age. But what God says is truth, and his Word did not come back void. Somewhere along the line, Abram chose to believe and his heart of belief, God said, made him righteous.

God, give me a believing heart. Help me to trust you and see your works both in my life and outside of it. Your works are proof of your existence. Surely the stars of heaven are bearing your testimony.

Cry Out to God

He lifted me out of the pit of despair,
out of the mud and the mire.
He set my feet on solid ground
and steadied me as I walked along.

PSALM 40:2 NIV

Emotions can be confusing. Sometimes they are a rollercoaster, and the ups and downs fly by faster than you can take in. Other times, you may feel like you've jumped into the deep end of a pool of sadness. You just sink and sink. When you are stuck in a pit of despair, cry out to God. He gave you your emotions, and he's aware of how you feel. No matter what, you can always cry out to him. He has compassion for you, and he wants to lift you up.

Jesus, I have no one else like you. No one else is there for me when my feet fail and my heart caves in. No one else is there for me like you are. You are a friend beyond any other, so I will praise you!

Prayers of Thanks

You know that I've been called to serve the God of my fathers with a clean conscience. Night and day I pray for you, thanking God for your life!

2 TIMOTHY 1:3 TPT

There are people in our lives that are like beacons of hope. Who cultivates gratitude in your heart? Which friends make you overflow with thanksgiving? Perhaps some have been steady supports in the tumultuous times of your life. Maybe a friend brings you laughter and joy when you need it most. Take some time to pray for these friends today, asking for their strength, encouragement, and breakthrough. Let gratitude lead you to the throne of your Father, and partner with his heart as you pray over your friends.

God, please watch over my family of believers! I pray over my brothers, over my sisters, and over all those who have blessed me by their spiritual maturity. Please watch over every one of them this day.

Sunshine and Storm

When times are good, be happy;
but when times are bad, consider this:
God has made the one as well as the other.
Therefore, no one can discover
anything about their future.

ECCLESIASTES 7:14 NIV

It's easy to feel happy on a sunny day, when all is well, the birds are singing, and life is going along swimmingly. But what happens when waters are rougher, bad news comes, or the days feel just plain hard? God has made each and every day. We are called to rejoice in all of them whether good or bad. Happiness is determined by our circumstances, but true joy comes when we can find the silver linings, hidden in our darkest hours—when we sing his praises no matter what. We don't know what the future holds for us here on earth, but we can find our delight in the knowledge that our eternity is set in beauty.

Whether in the rain or in the sunshine, I will praise you, Father in heaven. Surely it is the thunderstorm that causes the seed to spring forth and grow, so I will endure these rains as you use them to grow me.

Deep Yearning

"For this child I prayed, and the LORD has granted me my petition which I asked of Him. Therefore I also have lent him to the LORD; as long as he lives he shall be lent to the LORD."

1 SAMUEL 1:27-28 NKJV

Hannah grieved deeply because she had no children. In brokenness and despair, she went before the Lord and asked for a child. The Lord had mercy on her and granted her a son! Each of our stories is going to be different, but the lessons learned from Hannah's gratefulness and God's grace can be applied to any of us. Our Father does not owe us anything, yet he chooses to give good gifts. In reverent thankfulness we need to remember it was him who gave us the good gifts and see how we can use them for his service and praise.

God, all around me I see blessings. The very air in my lungs bears testimony of your love and providence. My life, my breath, gives me reason to trust in you. In the difficulty and the rejoicing, I will exult you.

Deserved Glory

"Why do you call me good?" Jesus asked him.
"No one is good except God alone."

MARK 10:18 CSB

Next to the perfection of God, our casual use of the term is convicting. Next to the most exquisite rose, God's brilliance would wither it. The loveliest face we've ever seen appears ordinary next to the beauty of the Lord. In all his humility, compassion, mercy, tenderness, and wisdom, Jesus declared himself unworthy next to God. How are we to comprehend such goodness, such perfection? Perhaps we are not. Perhaps we are meant only to celebrate it and to give him the glory he deserves.

God in Heaven, what is there that compares with you? Is there anything that can give me a picture of your glory, as unbound and infinite as it is? I can only honor you and worship you in adoration.

Despite Feelings

Why, my soul, are you downcast?
Why so disturbed within me?
Put your hope in God,
for I will yet praise him,
my Savior and my God.

PSALM 42:11 NIV

As you walk through days that are difficult, sometimes you might be just as discouraged by your reaction as you are by the actual cause of the difficulty. Perhaps you shy away from emotions that feel too big. Remember that you are given multiple examples in Scripture of men and women with passionate and raw reactions. Don't be discouraged by big feelings, put your hope in God. He is big enough for all of you, at your best and your worst.

God Almighty, how can I live with the weight in my chest? How can I live with all this hurt and pain? Please give me the strength to make it another day. On my own, I would drown in my emotion.

Despite What We Know

The apostles said to the Lord,
"Increase our faith."

LUKE 17:5 NLT

Every limitation we have is one designed by the Lord. Even the apostles, witness to every miracle and firsthand hearers of so much wisdom, needed more faith. It's one of the many things that remind us he is God, and we are not. He wants us to ask him for it. He loves to fill us with all the blessings of heaven, all the things we lack, and each time we pray for them, we acknowledge his greatness.

I will bring my requests to you this day, Lord. I will not hide what I am lacking. I will be honest about the things I cannot do on my own. I will ask you for what I do not have. I will ask you because there is none other who can provide for my every need.

Digging Holes

The trouble they cause recoils on them;
their violence comes down on their own heads.

PSALM 7:16 NIV

The next time you find yourself exhausted by the foolish actions of an unwise leader, take heart in knowing that there will be an end to their foolishness. People will not get away with consistently being manipulative and troublesome. Eventually their behavior catches up with them. Instead of finding words of abuse, pray for these people. Everyone is worthy of the restoration that Jesus brought into this world even if you don't feel they deserve it.

There is so much, Jesus, that I could choose to resent people for. There are so many ways I have been mistreated and harmed. Yet remind me that the punishment for their actions will fall on them and not on me. You are a just God, and I can trust you.

Distracted

The Spirit of the LORD will rest on him—
the Spirit of wisdom and understanding

ISAIAH 11:2 NLT

God isn't asking you to be perfect; he is the only perfect one.
He isn't alarmed by your inadequacies. He knew you would
sin, which is why he provided his Son as a sacrifice for you
to be restored to him when you confess. But there are simple
steps you can take to become a better person. Don't allow
distractions to hinder you from going to the one who has
every answer you could ever need.

*Holy Spirit, dwell in me this day. Teach me your ways and
give me the power to fight through every trial. I require your
strength, for on my own I am weak. I require your wisdom,
for without you I am foolish.*

Don't Stop

Never stop praying.

1 THESSALONIANS 5:17 NLT

Does praying come easily to you, or is it something that you struggle with? It is a spiritual discipline, sure, but there is no right or wrong way to pray. It is open communication with God, and he delights in hearing your voice. There is no need to feel pressure when it comes to talking to God. Simply talk to him like you would a close friend. Don't censor yourself with him. He has heard it all, and you can't offend him. Practice building up a habit of prayer in your daily life. Find a time where you can spend a few minutes talking to God. Whenever you think of it, pray, and see how it transforms you.

Lord, please teach me to live in prayer. Make into habit what is now only an aspiration, so that rather than being consumed by my own thoughts I might instead be built up by yours.

Draw Near

I am praying to you because I know you will answer, O God.
Bend down and listen as I pray.

PSALM 17:6 NLT

What a wonderful, inexpressible reality it is that God hears
us when we turn to him. He always does! When we don't
know where else to turn, let us approach him. When we are
at a loss for what to do, let's pray to him. He is faithful in love,
and he will never turn away from us in our need. He will not
just hear us; he will answer us. Every time. He is that good. In
fact, he is better than we can imagine. What a beautiful God
he is. Let's not hold back a single thing from him today. There
is an open line of communication here and now.

*I need you to reach down to my level and hear me. Should I
ascend to heaven? Surely, I could not if I tried. Please, God,
out of your abundant mercy and humility, lean down to me
and hear my prayer.*

Not in a Box

The LORD is near to all who call on him,
yes, to all who call on him in truth.

PSALM 145:18 NLT

If things don't turn out the way we have planned, does
that mean that God hasn't answered our prayers? We can't
simplify our life and prayers and God like that. When we do,
we put God in a box—where he does not belong. God is not
our great genie in the sky, granting wishes or denying them.
Prayer is a part of your relationship with God. It strengthens
your faith, exposes your weaknesses, and leads to real
communion with the Father.

*In my pain, you are there. In my rejoicing, you are there.
You are always there, Jesus, through thick and thin, feasting
and fasting. You are an ever-faithful companion, and I can
always rely on you.*

Dwelling Within

Nevertheless, turn Your attention to the prayer of Your servant and to his plea, Lord, my God, to listen to the cry and to the prayer which Your servant prays before You today, so that Your eyes may be open toward this house night and day, toward the place of which You have said, 'My name shall be there,' to listen to the prayer which Your servant will pray toward this place.

1 KINGS 8:28-29 NASB

Solomon had spent such a long time devoting the best for a temple in which to worship God. He knew that heaven itself couldn't contain the greatness of God, yet he believed that God would still allow his presence to be near those who truly came to worship him. When you take the time to think of yourself as this temple, it can be humbling to know that God dwells within you despite your lack of effort to make it a great place to worship. Praise Jesus that he makes this temple a beautiful place.

God, please open your heart to me. Know my emotions and my thoughts, so clearly and so perfectly. Be near to me, and I will take your hand to lead me from death to life.

Each New Morning

Tell me in the morning about your love,
because I trust you.
Show me what I should do,
because my prayers go up to you

PSALM 143:8 NCV

There are many verses in the Bible that talk about morning prayer. Jesus himself set an example by getting up early and going to a quiet place to pray and talk with God. There is something about the morning that God values. Mornings symbolize new life, strong hope, and fresh beginnings—all things that we know God is passionate about. When we seek God in the morning, we consecrate the first moments of the day. By coming and placing ourselves at his feet before we do anything else, we put him first in our hearts, souls, and minds.

God, I need you so desperately! Minister to my spirit by your Holy Spirit, so that I might rely on you. My place is at your feet, and my greatest aspiration is to feel the warmth of your presence.

Embrace the Day

The LORD is my strength and my defense;
he has become my salvation.
He is my God, and I will praise him,
my father's God, and I will exalt him.

EXODUS 15:2 NIV

How we start our day can make all the difference in our attitude and outlook on life. A healthy breakfast, some exercise, and a relaxing routine are great ways to start, but what do our souls need? Rolling out of bed, we can grumble about having to finish an assignment, complain that we have to spend the day at work, or get upset that we have to run errands. Or we can choose to wake with praise and gratitude for a new day. We have so much to be thankful for, and that thanks is due to God. Recognizing that every day is a gift gives us a fresh perspective. Instead of dreading the day ahead, we can embrace it with hope and joy.

Father God, sustainer of life, I choose optimism today. I choose to trust in you! I choose to rejoice rather than despair because you have saved me from the hell I deserve. Thank you.

May

I pray that your hearts will be flooded with light so that you can understand the confident hope he has given to those he called—his holy people who are his rich and glorious inheritance.

EPHESIANS 1:18 NLT

Encouragement

Anxiety in a person's heart weighs it down,
but a good word cheers it up.

PROVERBS 12:25 CSB

When anxieties overwhelm your senses, what do you do? There are as many coping mechanisms as there are people in this world. When you are faced with the unknown, practice turning to Jesus. The more you do it, the more natural it will become. When you are filled with worry, you can take it all to God in prayer. He has plentiful, perfect peace to calm your anxious thoughts.

Lord, I cannot live with the weight of this worry and anxiety. I have been brought low by a burden I was never made to shoulder. Please cheer up my heart! Let your living water quench my thirsty soul.

Enduring Kingdom

Everyone praise the Lord God of Israel,
always and forever!
For he is from eternity past
and will remain for the eternity to come.
That's the way it will be forever.
Faithful is our King! Amen!

PSALM 41:13 TPT

When Israel pictured an eternal kingdom, they were thinking of a physical kingdom, something like they had known but stronger and more powerful. God, however, had a plan that went beyond a kingdom made with human hands. His kingdom was not made from iron, bronze, clay, silver, or gold, but in the person of Jesus Christ, who started a kingdom that could never be destroyed. Remember that this is the kingdom you are a part of now and praise God that the best is yet to come.

Lord of Hosts, you alone will endure. Surely, the things which cling to you shall last, and everything apart from you will not last. With the host of saints and angels, bring me with you into eternity!

Enemies

"Love your enemies, and do good, and lend, expecting
nothing in return, and your reward will be great, and you
will be sons of the Most High, for he is kind to the ungrateful
and the evil."

LUKE 6:35 ESV

Jesus asks us to be kind to our enemies. This is not easy. You
might not think you have any enemies, but you don't need to
declare war to place someone in the enemy camp. It might be
that guy that you scroll past on social media, the man at the
Bible study who has all the right answers, or the co-worker
who glares at you. One way to start practicing kindness
toward those you don't get along with is through prayer. Say
a prayer for them, or simply speak their name in prayer to
Jesus if you can't find good words. Watch God work in your
heart and in that relationship.

*Most High God, make me your child in my words and
actions. Let them reflect your character, so those around me
would see the way I live and praise your name!*

Enemy Tactic

Let them all be glad,
those who turn aside to hide themselves in you.
May they keep shouting for joy forever!
Overshadow them in your presence
as they sing and rejoice,
then every lover of your name
will burst forth with endless joy.

PSALM 5:11 TPT

The more you dive into your relationship with the Lord, the more the enemy will want to pull you away. The more you begin to listen for God's voice, the more Satan will try to whisper in your ear. Allowing yourself to become closer to God is the last thing the enemy wants for you. Don't believe the lies! God wants you to be filled with joy and peace, and that is what he offers you as you draw near to him.

As Satan and his angels fire their flaming arrows, you alone, Jesus, can protect me! The shield of faith, the God of refuge, is surely my shelter in the turbulence of every storm.

Eternal Song

I will sing to the LORD all my life;
I will sing praise to my God as long as I live.

PSALM 104:33 NIV

Not only do we get to express ourselves to our Creator in this life, but we will continue to share our joys and concerns with him into eternity. You might be thinking that eventually we would run out of songs to sing, or poems to write, or messages to teach. But think of all the songs you have heard in your lifetime. Each one is different: there are no songs that have the exact same lyrics, let alone melody! We serve a creative God that illuminates his creativity throughout humanity. Enjoy that unique expression and offer it up to the Lord today.

Gracious Lord Jesus, thank you for the promise of eternity! Thank you for assuring that my praise will ever be lifted up to you. I pray today that you would give me a heart of thanksgiving.

Free My Soul

Free me from my prison,
and then I will praise your name.
Then good people will surround me,
because you have taken care of me.

PSALM 142:7 NCV

Nobody likes the thought of being stuck in something they can't get out of. You don't have to have been trapped in an elevator to know what it would feel like to not be in control of your freedom. The truth is that Jesus came to set you free. He does not want you to be in a prison of any description. When you ask for a breakthrough, expect freedom, and then be ready to encourage other believers with what he has done for you.

God, why have these prison bars sprung up around me?
Why have I found my freedom lacking and my feet shackled?
Break these chains! Break them and set me free.

Even in Bed

Let those who worship him
rejoice in his glory.
Let them sing for joy even in bed!

PSALM 149:5 NCV

The Israelites would often have very arduous rituals to seek out the presence of God. What a joy it must have been to know that God could be praised from one's own bed! You may have gotten out of bed already but take some time to appreciate that you can approach your loving King in the comfort of your own room. Jesus has made a way to make his home in your heart, so be mindful of his presence within you today.

Every second of this day is yours, Lord. Whether at work or at rest, I am in a position to praise your name. May the meditation of my heart be on your Word, so I would grow closer to you.

Even Though

Even though the fig trees have no blossoms,
and there are no grapes on the vines;
even though the olive crop fails,
and the fields lie empty and barren…
yet I will rejoice in the LORD!
I will be joyful in the God of my salvation!

HABAKKUK 3:17-18 NLT

When nothing seems to be going right, do we still rejoice in the Lord? This is when praise can be a sacrifice: offering what we do not readily have to give in the moment because the one who receives it deserves it. God is as good in the drought as he is in the harvest. He is as faithful in winter as he is in summer. He is loyal in love, always providing for our needs. Let's offer him our praise both in and out of season. Let's never stop telling of his wonderful nature!

Lord and Savior, how great is your faithfulness! Surely, you will never forsake me nor forget me. I know that I can trust my every need with you because even the hairs on my head are counted by you.

There He Is

"Where two or three are gathered in my name,
there am I among them."

MATTHEW 18:20 ESV

Jesus promised to be present any time his followers gathered together in his name, and he is. You've felt it, haven't you? There is such beauty in friendships born of faith, such a sacred tenderness to the way the body of Christ looks after one another's hearts; it could only be the loving presence of Jesus. Gathering in pursuit of Christ—to know him, to worship him, or to serve him—is to find him. He brings with him a love that transcends age, economics, and worldly interests and unites us in our love for him. Wherever we are, there he is and wherever he is, there is love.

God, I pray today that you would bring me into the presence of fellow believers. I pray that we would be united through our love for you, and that your presence would be felt among us.

Everlasting Contentment

Make sure that your character is free from the love of money,
being content with what you have; for He Himself has said,
"I will never desert you, nor will I ever abandon you."

HEBREWS 13:5 NASB

Those who are led around by a love for money will never
know contentment in Christ. They will be easily led and
manipulated because money is fickle and easy to lose.
Security cannot be found in money; it can only be found
in God who faithfully promises to never forsake us. Wealth
can give no such assurance. If we make lots of money in our
obedience to God and in using the gifts which he has given
us, then let us use that money to praise him and love others.
If we make barely enough to get by, let us continue to praise
him and find everlasting contentment in his grace.

*When money is tight, what I have is still yours. You are to be
praised in times of prosperity, and you are to be praised in
times of thrift. I will entrust my needs to you, Lord, because
you can be counted on.*

Everyone Talking

Your awe-inspiring acts of power have everyone talking!
And I'm telling people everywhere about your excellent
greatness!

PSALM 145:6 TPT

If you could brag on a friend in any way, telling others about
the amazing traits they uphold, what would you say? What
do you want your friends to say about you? If they were to
describe what makes you a good friend, what would they
say? If there seems to be a disconnect between what you
want to be true and what seems to be true, take some time to
put intention into action. You can change how you show up
in relationships. Even small movements and shifts matter.

*God, please make me someone who is of good repute and
beloved by my brothers and sisters in the church. May I be
someone who tells of your good works rather than just my
difficulties and trials.*

Juggling Act

The answer is, if you eat or drink,
or if you do anything,
do it all for the glory of God.

1 CORINTHIANS 10:31 NCV

Most of us are busy. We pack our schedules with commitments, obligations, necessities, rewards, and—hopefully—rest. Like an expert juggler, we toss in one more ball, then another, until one drops. Scrambling to retrieve it, we also risk those still in the air. These are ideal opportunities to check in and ask why we are juggling so much. If we desire to live a God-honoring life, we should make meaningful use of our time: giving, serving, experiencing community, and stewarding our responsibilities. When our motive is to do everything for God, he helps us with the juggling act.

Lord, may I not be a slave to schedules and agendas. Make my time your own: a gift given to you in recognition of your lordship and sovereignty over my life.

Everything Made Right

I will give all my thanks to you, Lord,
for you make everything right in the end.
I will sing my highest praise to the God of the Highest Place!

PSALM 7:17 TPT

No matter where we are in our journey, whether it's in the messy middle of a transition or in the beginning of a new venture, God will make everything right in the end. Even when we think we are at our end, if it isn't right or good, it's not the end of what God is doing. We cannot escape trouble or trials. We already know this to be true. And we cannot control how our lives will end. But even when our bodies fail us, God is not done working. We will know incomparable joy, peace, love, and satisfaction in the fullness of his kingdom in eternity.

In the valleys and on the mountains, I know you are working. Lord, I have heard that all things work for the good of those who love you, so I pray that you would teach me to trust in your path.

Exalted

"Give praise to the LORD, proclaim his name;
make known among the nations what he has done,
and proclaim that his name is exalted."

ISAIAH 12:4 NIV

What is truly worthy of exultation? We love to promote our accomplishments: our education, our job, or our many acquaintances. Maybe we lift up others in our lives who have done great things. Whatever we do, and whomever we glorify, are they more worthy of our praise than God? We should make known to the nations the praises and practices of our God. He has done glorious things that we should exclaim to others.

God of wonders, maker of galaxies, and destroyer of empires, who can compare with you in your majesty? I stand amazed when I consider your perfect strength and humility.

Exciting Adventure

Since the world began, no ear has heard and no eye has seen
a God like you, who works for those who wait for him!

ISAIAH 64:4 NLT

Being a believer is not just another title to throw on the list
of roles you hold. It should be a completely life-changing
experience, affecting all areas of your reality. The Christian
life is quite the adventure for the one who submits to God's
will. God gives each of us specific spiritual gifts; have you
discovered yours? Looking into this can bring clarity and
vitality to your life. If you wrote down your prayers and
revisited them at a later date, you would find a pathway of all
the incredible ways God showed up.

*I know you are working, Lord. I know that you are a God
who helps those who wait upon you, and that gives me hope.
Work wondrously this day, and I will praise you and tell of
your good works!*

Expressions of Praise

The trumpeters and musicians joined in unison to give praise and thanks to the LORD. Accompanied by trumpets, cymbals and other instruments, the singers raised their voices in praise to the LORD and sang: "He is good; his love endures forever."

2 CHRONICLES 5:13 NIV

There is rarely a Christian church where a service is not accompanied with some form of music and singing. It is a part of our humanity to express ourselves through music, and it is part of our faith to express our praise in song. It doesn't matter if you can play an instrument or sing along to the tune, God delights in you raising your voice as an expression of your for him. What a beautiful sound it must be to him when his children sing together and acknowledge his goodness.

God, I pray today that you would give me new and meaningful ways to praise your name! May I worship you in the small moments of the day with my choices and my faithfulness in the little matters of life.

Filled with Cloud

The temple of the LORD was filled with the cloud, and the priests could not perform their service because of the cloud, for the glory of the LORD filled the temple of God.

2 CHRONICLES 5:14 NIV

God's presence is always with us, but sometimes there are some significant moments when his presence fills a whole room, and everybody feels it. Have you had the chance this week to worship with other believers? Find some time to add this into your week so you can experience God in a new and refreshing way. Let go of some of the distractions and barriers that prevent you from really expressing your gratitude and joy for the God of creation who loves you so much.

Lord, please fill my mind with your presence. Open up my heart and let me see the wonders you have wrought both within me and outside of me. I praise you, Lord, for there is none like you in majesty and power!

Extent of Love

For this reason I kneel before the Father, from whom every family in heaven and on earth derives its name. I pray that out of his glorious riches he may strengthen you with power through his Spirit in your inner being, so that Christ may dwell in your hearts through faith. And I pray that you, being rooted and established in love, may have power, together with all the Lord's holy people, to grasp how wide and long and high and deep is the love of Christ, and to know this love that surpasses knowledge—that you may be filled to the measure of all the fullness of God.

EPHESIANS 3:14-19 NIV

Paul's letter written to the Ephesians was a powerful prayer that sprang from his deep desire to see the people living a life that was only achieved with total commitment to Christ. He believed that it was worth the struggle that often came with living this way, because the reward was great. This letter could've been written to each and every one of us. When we feel Christ's indwelling in our hearts, we can experience true power, and true love.

God of love and mercy, reach down from your throne to touch my heart. Help me to fathom how deep your love is! if I would like to love others as you did, I have only to understand your love.

Eyes Open

Since we are approaching the end of all things,
be intentional, purposeful, and self-controlled
so that you can be given to prayer.

1 PETER 4:7 TPT

There is wisdom in being sober minded about the times we
are living in. Sober minded doesn't mean overly serious, for
there is joy to be found in the presence of our God and King.
However, it requires living with intention, purpose, and self-
control. Let us build lifestyles of prayer. We have unrestricted
access to God the Father. There is not a moment where we
cannot fully and openly communicate with him. May we
learn to turn our attention to him as often as we think of
it. In all things, on all occasions, with eyes wide open, offer
your attention to God through constant communion.

*God, sanctify my vision and my perception. Let me see this
world in light of the eternity awaiting all of us, and may I be
sober in that reality. I pray that you would help me to walk
in faith at all times.*

Face of Jesus

When I saw him, I fell at his feet as though dead. But he laid
his right hand on me, saying, "Fear not, I am the first and
the last, and the living one. I died, and behold I am alive
forevermore, and I have the keys of Death and Hades."

REVELATION 1:17-18 ESV

The Jesus who walked this earth and ate with his disciples
is a bit different from the Jesus we find in Revelation. John
writes that he fell at Jesus' feet as though dead because the
sight of him was so glorious. The Bible talks about Jesus' eyes
being like flames of fire and his hair being as white as wool.
It describes the rainbow of living color that surrounds his
throne. What a picture! Jesus is magnificently wonderful, and
words cannot describe the awe we will feel when we are face
to face with him. Praise him today for his wonderful power.

*Jesus, how great you are in majesty and power! You are the
Lion of Judah, and the Lamb who was slain. You are perfect
in all measures, and none can manage to stand before your
glory and radiance!*

Faithful Direction

I will instruct you and teach you in the way you should go;
I will counsel you with my loving eye on you
PSALM 32:8 NIV

There is no right way to arrange a household. Some homes might have a stay-at-home-parent, others have two working parents, and still others have single parents leading the charge. Whatever the situation, passion must be involved— for work, for children, or for the home. If that passion has yet to reveal itself, pray. In order to hear what calling God has placed on our lives, we have to listen. And it can take a while. Fully understanding what God wants us to do with our lives can take years, and certain pieces of our calling might only surface for a season. When our hearts are radically changed, and we become passionate about a possibility, then we might have found a clue to our calling.

Heavenly Father, I pray today for instruction. I pray that you would instruct me and teach me your path. Hold my hand, guide my feet, and keep me near to you. Only through you can I manage to not stumble.

Faithful Forever

Praise the LORD, all you nations;
extol him, all you peoples.
For great is his love toward us,
and the faithfulness of the LORD endures forever.
Praise the LORD.

PSALM 117:1-2 NIV

Although this is the shortest Psalm in the Bible, its impact is still immense. It testifies of who God is; how loving and faithful he is. In response to his greatness, it instructs us to praise him. The Lord is faithful forever, and by his great love he has saved anyone from any nation who is willing to give their life to him. The application of this abundant grace is appropriate: praise him!

Lord, I give you my heart, whole and undivided. Please take it and be glorified through my service and my acceptance of your service toward me. I praise you, for you are faithful in providence and mercy.

Fast and Strong

His pleasure is not in the strength of the horse,
  nor his delight in the legs of the warrior;
the LORD delights in those who fear him,
  who put their hope in his unfailing love.

PSALM 147:10-11 NIV

As impressive as it is to see an athlete's grace, to hear a singer's unique tone, or to behold a craftsman's handiwork, how much more moved are we by acts of generosity and compassion? God gave us our unique talents and attributes, and he wants us to use them, but his heart doesn't sing when we do; it sings when we sing to him. He's not moved by your talent; he's moved by your trust. It is not your way with words that delights him, but the words you use to honor him. He wants your devotion.

God, why do I always fall back into the old habit of glorifying myself? Why do I continually neglect to give you glory for what you have done? I pray this day that you would teach me to put my hope in your unfailing love and to praise you for it.

Father Time

Daniel…went home to his upstairs room where the windows opened toward Jerusalem. Three times a day he got down on his knees and prayed, giving thanks to his God, just as he had done before.

DANIEL 6:10 NIV

Even though Daniel was a slave, he was one of the most powerful men in the kingdom. The king had given him power over all Babylon. Daniel was responsible for a lot of people, so he had a busy schedule. But still Daniel went to his room three times a day, got down on his knees, and prayed. That very important man knew what was most important in his day—spending time with God.

Father God, please help me to see that no priority compares to being with you. May my heart long for your glorious presence, and may I find the precious time to rest in it.

Discover Peace

You will keep in perfect peace
all who trust in you,
all whose thoughts are fixed on you!

ISAIAH 26:3 NLT

What does chaos look like in your world? Crazy work deadlines, over-scheduled activities, long to-do lists and short hours? All of the above? How about peace? What does that look like? Most of us immediately picture having gotten away, whether to the master bathroom tub or a sunny beach. It's quiet. Serene. The trouble with that image, lovely as it is, is that it's fleeting. We can't live in our bathtubs or in Fiji, so our best bet is to seek out peace right in the middle of our chaos. Guess what? We can have it. Jesus promises peace to all who put him first.

You are peace, Lord! Take my mind and make it your temple. Let my thoughts continually be turned toward you in devotion and faith. Without you, God, my mind is a place of darkness and despair.

Finding Words

I will rejoice and be glad in Your faithfulness,
Because You have seen my misery;
You have known the troubles of my soul.

PSALM 31:7 NASB

Do you ever sit down to pray and find yourself struggling to find words? You stumble over your words; your mind draws a blank. You want to be obedient by spending time with the Lord, but you don't even know where to begin. When you find yourself searching for the right way to express what you want to say to God, know that he will intercede if you allow him to. Spend some time sitting quietly and let him take the reins for you today. He knows the troubles of your soul.

You are not a far-off deity. You do not remove yourself from my pain, nor do you choose to isolate yourself from discomfort. You are here, Lord, in my misery, and I praise you for that. You, and only you, are a perfectly true friend in times of trouble.

Sunrise Reflections

We all, with unveiled face, beholding the glory of the Lord,
are being transformed into the same image from
one degree of glory to another. For this comes
from the Lord who is the Spirit.

2 CORINTHIANS 3:18 ESV

Sunrises are always beautiful. Few are as gorgeous as the sun coming up over a body of water. The pinkish orange glow rises over the shimmering waves, and the world begins to come alive. Part of the beauty occurs when the sun is at just the right angle for the water to reflect its brilliance. If we stay close to God by reading his Word and talking to him often, we will be ready to reflect his love to a world that desperately needs him.

Lord, I pray today that I would be transformed into your image. I pray that you would take my mortal mind and soul and make them eternal, changing them from the imprint of this world into the image of the eternal God.

Forgiveness

"If you forgive those who sin against you, your heavenly
Father will forgive you. But if you refuse to forgive others,
your Father will not forgive your sins."

MATTHEW 6:14–15 NLT

Jesus was very practical in his advice to his followers.
Though he often spoke in parables and stories, he also gave
clear direction and application. After he taught his disciples
to pray (what we know as the Lord's Prayer), he instructed
them to forgive those who had wronged them. This remains
true for us. Let us not overlook this important point.
When we forgive others, God forgives us. We should never
withhold forgiveness, for it will be to our own detriment.

*Holy Spirit, within my soul there lies resentment which
I must let go of. Without your strength, I cannot pardon
a single offense, no matter how slight. I pray that you
would empower me to offer forgiveness, unequivocally and
undeserved.*

Joy

The joyful shouting and weeping mingled together in a loud noise that could be heard far in the distance.

EZRA 3:13 NLT

What a noise it must have been for a whole nation's weeping and joyful shouting to be heard from far off. It would be like hearing a stadium erupt when a team scores. It's amazing the kind of impact people can have when they are gathered together to celebrate. God receives all expressions of praise. You might be someone who likes to shout at the top of your lungs when you are full of joy, or perhaps you are more moved to happy tears. God loves it all.

Lord Jesus, I pray that my eyes would see the congregation of your people gathered together in joyful praise and sorrowful mourning. Whatever the feeling, God, I pray that we would feel it together.

Fragrant Offering

Let my prayer be as the evening sacrifice
that burns like fragrant incense,
rising as my offering to you
as I lift up my hands in surrendered worship!

PSALM 141:2 TPT

Wherever this finds you, no matter the greatness of your joy or the depth of your despair, may you take the opportunity to lift your prayer to God as an offering to him. Don't withhold your attention or your experience. Let your prayer rise with surrendered worship to the one who knows you well. David penned these words with an urgent need for God's help. If you are desperate for God's help, press into him. Turn your heart to the Lord. He is near.

Lord, today I give you what I am feeling. Whether I have joy or despair, I offer it to you in humility and thanksgiving. Please take these emotions and sanctify them with your blood.

Free from Chains

His light broke through the darkness
and he led us out in freedom from death's dark shadow
and snapped every one of our chains.

PSALM 107:14 TPT

We need to hear the truth of Christ's promise for us and stop the cycle of hopelessness, defeat, and bondage to sin. All we need to do is get on our knees and pray. Wait for God's voice to permeate the deepest, saddest parts of you, and let him snap every one of those chains that tries to hold you in darkness. He wants you to let him take care of you. He is pursuing your heart.

God, when the darkness is real to me, you are so much greater. I am surrounded by enemies, yet I know a host of allies exists around me. Give me faith in the strength of your arm.

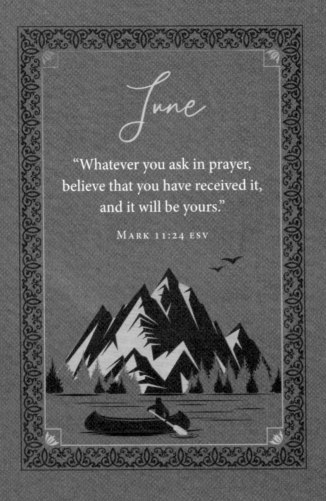

June

"Whatever you ask in prayer,
believe that you have received it,
and it will be yours."

MARK 11:24 ESV

Freed by Love

He did rescue us from mortal danger,
and he will rescue us again.
We have placed our confidence in him,
and he will continue to rescue us.

2 CORINTHIANS 1:10 NLT

God moves through the prayers of his people. Just as he wants us to cry out to him, we should also cry out for each other. He is pleased when we work together and lift up each other's burdens. He loves to answer his children, and there are so many in your circle of influence who need your prayer. You could be asking for deliverance for them right now. Join in their cry, and watch God move mountains!

You are the God of refuge. You are my port in every storm, my shield in every battle, my hope in every trial. Please deliver me today from the foes I face, for my confidence is in you alone.

From the Heart

"A time is coming and has now come when the true worshipers will worship the Father in the Spirit and in truth, for they are the kind of worshipers the Father seeks."

JOHN 4:23 NIV

When Jesus met the woman at the well, she questioned him about the right place to worship. As a Samaritan woman, her people worshipped on a certain mountain and the Jews worshipped on another. Jesus' answer might have seemed perplexing, but he was getting to the heart of the matter. Now that God had appeared to the world in the flesh, worship was not about ritual, culture, or place. Jesus pushed beyond the boundaries to reveal that worship comes from within. You have the opportunity to worship God wherever you are today.

May I be the worshiper you seek, Father. May I live in a posture of humility and kindness, searching for your sovereignty's rule in me. Come and display your glory through me!

Fulfilled Hopes

Hope deferred makes the heart sick,
but a desire fulfilled is a tree of life.

PROVERBS 13:12 ESV

Embrace the opportunity to lay out all your hopes before
the Lord. He is near, he is listening, and he welcomes your
honest pleas. Don't hold back any request. Jesus encouraged
his disciples to ask in faith without holding back. Seize
the freedom and confidence that is yours and pour out
your heart to him. Whatever your hopes, find strength to
persevere in the waiting. There is more than enough grace.
There is fullness of love, peace, and joy.

*At your right hand there are pleasures forever, merciful Lord.
Please, build in me a hope that lasts, but also let me see my
heart's desires fulfilled before my eyes. I wait upon you with
longing and faith.*

Full Attention

Answer me when I call, O God of my righteousness!
You have given me relief when I was in distress.
Be gracious to me and hear my prayer!

PSALM 4:1 ESV

Tensions seem to be high for our psalmist, with stress mounting up all around him. How does the king deal with the stress? He turns to prayer. Prayer is the greatest stress reliever in our lives. It's not so much what happens after we pray, but rather the presence of the one to whom we pray. The relief comes when we notice that we have God's attention. He hears, he answers, and he cares.

Lord God, please hear my cry! I have no other master or hope to trust in but you, so where else will I go? You are my refuge, so please hear me when I pray to you with humility and patience.

Fully Restored

He forgives all my sins
and heals all my diseases.

PSALM 103:3 NCV

When you are spiritually or physically weak, it's easy to forget the promises of God. In these times, think on his character; remember that he is a loving father who wants the best for you. Praise him with all of your heart, soul, and mind and watch him bring restoration to the areas of your life in which you need it the most.

God of restoration, please work your way in me. Take the burdens that weigh on my back and slip them off. Heal the brokenness in my heart and mind, so I can better help those around me.

Gaining Understanding

Joyful is the person who finds wisdom,
the one who gains understanding.

PROVERBS 3:13 NLT

We are not in a giant game of hide-and-seek. What a relief!
Wisdom is not hiding from you. If you feel you are lacking
in wisdom, or if you don't know where to find it, the answer
is right here. If you need wisdom, James tells us to ask for it.
Have you asked God for the wisdom you need lately? Have
you listened for an answer? Spending time in God's Word is
a great way to stock up on wisdom. Then, when you ask, the
Holy Spirit can draw from the deep reservoir you have created
within yourself of God's Word and remind you of the truth.

*Lord of all wisdom, guide me and instruct my heart in the
way of life. Write your words on my conscience, so I would
not stray from your path but would point others in the
direction of your Word instead.*

Get Up and Pray

Very early in the morning, while it was still dark, Jesus got up, left the house and went off to a solitary place, where he prayed.

MARK 1:35 NIV

Jesus did not rely on his own strength to get through the day; he made it a priority to spend time with his Father before he did anything else. He was not doing it out of obligation but out of a living relationship. He came from the Father, and he knew he needed the Father's perspective to help him in all things. We can take Jesus' example and start our days with prayer. Whatever is on our hearts, minds, and schedules is an open invitation for God's perspective, help, and power when we communicate it to him.

Lord, I need time alone with you today. Please provide me a space of solitude to reach you and converse with you. This world is full of confusion, but you make things clear through your Word.

Glad for Each Day

This is the day that the LORD has made;
let us rejoice and be glad in it.
PSALM 118:24 ESV

Every single day of our lives is an opportunity to rejoice
and be glad. If God made it, it is good. He created time,
with each day representing a testimony to his goodness. The
psalmist is among the smartest of people if he knew that
God was worthy of praise for his works. Every morning we
wake up, we can look outside and see the sky. We can feel
the wind, the ground beneath our feet, and watch the sun
as it describes the course of the day. Every aspect of our day
is created by the same Creator. The joy and gladness of the
Lord runs deeper than the cares and trials of the world.

*Lord, you have provided for this world so greatly! Thank you
for this day, for the air I breathe, and for the ground beneath
my feet. I praise you for all these things, and for the people
that you have placed around me.*

Glorious Meditation

On the glorious splendor of your majesty,
and on your wondrous works, I will meditate.

PSALM 145:5 NLT

When we take time to meditate on the tangible goodness of
God, our hearts expand in his incredible mercy. The Lord is
more glorious than our minds can comprehend at any given
moment. He is larger than our little lives can contain. He
is purer than the most well-intentioned act of love we have
ever known. Let's take time to meditate on his wondrous
works. As we remember who he is, what he has done, and
what he has promised to do, may our hearts bloom with
hope. He is so very good and always worthy of our praise,
our time, and our attention.

*Precious Jesus, I desire your presence in my life. I pray that
your splendor and wondrous works would be ever before me,
in my mind and on my heart. May they remind me of your
faithfulness and mercy.*

Grace and Glory

The LORD God is our sun and our shield.
He gives us grace and glory.
The LORD will withhold no good thing
from those who do what is right.

PSALM 84:11 NLT

How beautiful that you serve a God who gives you grace and glory. Not only does he empower you to live rightly but then he rewards you for it even though it is his work within you that has made you holy. He is the God who delights in providing for you, protecting you, and encouraging you. He is your sun, the source of your life, and the one who sustains you. When you follow him, he says that he will withhold no good thing from you. Praise him today for all he has done in your life and in your heart.

God, what was I before you? You have taken a poor sinner and slowly but surely crafted me into your image. Help me to better appreciate just what you have done for me from the foundations of the earth.

Glory Origin

In your glory and grandeur go forth in victory!
Through your faithfulness and meekness
the cause of truth and justice will stand.
Awe-inspiring miracles are accomplished by your power,
leaving everyone dazed and astonished!

PSALM 45:4 TPT

When we achieve great things, it can become easy to forget where our successes come from. We worked so hard; we did so much to earn it! There is nothing wrong with climbing the ladder of success, but when we neglect to give the honor to God for all of our achievements, we lose sight of the victory itself. Instead, we should do it all for the glory of God. He is the one who gives us all that we have.

To you, God, do I ascribe all the glory! It is your hand that has established my every victory and caused me to succeed. May your name be praised today and forevermore.

He Heard Me

Certainly God has heard me;
He has attended to the voice of my prayer.
PSALM 66:19 NKJV

If you've ever felt lost in a crowd, alone in your thoughts, or misunderstood, then you know how powerful it is when someone truly listens to you. We all want to be heard and understood. Praying may sometimes seem one-sided, but it isn't. God hears every word we whisper and even the ones we don't. Our Maker loves us completely. We are not drowned out by grander prayers elsewhere; he leans in and listens to every cry of our hearts because he cares deeply about his children. He attends to us. We may not always see the results, but our loving Father remains with us.

Like a perfect wind surrounding me, you have swept me up in your love, Lord. You hear my every cry, my every laugh. You are near to me in the pain when all others, even my closest friends, abandon me. Thank you!

The Creation

Splendid and majestic is His work,
And His righteousness endures forever.
PSALM 111:3 NASB

Incredible sights, like a massive canyon or towering mountain peaks, make it hard to deny that there is a vastly intelligent creator. When you stop to smell the fragrance of a budding rose or watch a colony of ants as they busily scurry, you cannot refute that this earth and its inhabitants are the result of the most creative mind in existence. At the first cry of a newborn babe, we bow to the brilliance and intricacy knitted together by the hands of the designer of life. There is no doubt in the minds of believers that everything on this earth was made by God Almighty. All that he made will praise his holy name.

There is no other besides you, Lord. No one else deserves your glory; no one else deserves your praise. I love you, for you have lifted me up from corruption to adoption in you, and your righteousness washes over me.

God's Goodness

I remain confident of this:
I will see the goodness of the LORD
in the land of the living.

PSALM 27:13 NIV

How can we experience the goodness of God in our lives? Have a love for God's Word. Know it well. Being familiar with the promises of God will empower you to see him acting, and it will build faith that he is true to who he says he is. Have a right view of his nature. Culture, upbringing, and experience can sometimes skew our perceptions of God. We must make sure that how we view him is in line with how he truly is. Live expectant for God to move and speak as you create space in your life for worship and prayer. The goodness of God will become more evident to you as you walk closely with him.

Nearer to you, Lord, I want to be nearer to you! I want to walk alongside you, feeling your presence in every decision and choice I am presented with. Be my companion when friends desert me.

Good Hearts

God protects me like a shield;
he saves those whose hearts are right.

PSALM 7:10 NCV

We can go through all the right Christian expectations:
attending church, fasting, tithing, serving on the music or
children's team. We can help out with missions and take
communion or recite liturgy. All of these are excellent
Christian disciplines, but we need to examine our heart
motivations for why we are doing them. If you seek these
things for praise from others, or because it somehow fills
your expectations, then they aren't worth a whole lot to God.
He wants you to be motivated to do things for him because
you love just as he does.

*Father, you are a refuge for those who run to you! I pray
today over those who lay destroyed by sin and the devil. I
pray for you to rescue their souls and bring them into your
holy family.*

Stored Goodness

"Things which eye has not seen and ear has not heard,
And which have not entered the human heart,
All that God has prepared for those who love Him."

1 CORINTHIANS 2:9 NASB

There is no one like Jesus in the whole world, nor will there ever be. He is full of wisdom, full of pure and loyal love, full of kindness, full of truth, full of joy. The wonders of his nature would never be rightly contained in our praise. He is so much better than we could ever give him credit for. And he loves us! His love is complete, purifying our hearts in his mercy. Ask him to reveal more of himself to you today.

Lord, I pray my eyes would be turned to the glory awaiting me. I pray that you would give me hope in the fire and faith in the trial. Please remind me of the things which you are preparing for me beyond all comparison.

Great Love

As high as the heavens are above the earth,
so great is his steadfast love toward those who fear him.

PSALM 103:11 NIV

Did you know it would take the fastest spaceship almost ten years to travel to Pluto? That's pretty far away, and it's just a dwarf planet. There is so much more to God's vast and marvelous universe, and this is how great the Bible says his love is for us! He is a truly wonderful God. Is there a way you can show your respect for such an amazing Creator today?

Create in me a reverent heart, God. May I give you the respect and love which your majesty asks of me. How could anything in creation compare to the Father of all creation?

Good and Faithful

"His master replied, 'Well done, good and faithful servant!
You have been faithful with a few things;
I will put you in charge of many things.
Come and share your master's happiness!'"

MATTHEW 25:23 NIV

Well done. Good. Faithful. These are powerful affirmations coming from the master at the conclusion of the parable of the talents. He had given three servants each a different amount of money according to their abilities. Upon his return, he found that two of the servants had doubled his money which pleased him very much. They were offered promotions and a share in his happiness. The third servant buried his money, making nothing, and he suffered dire consequences. God has entrusted us with valuable commodities to use for his kingdom. We should invest in the lives of others for the glory of God. The return may only be revealed in heaven—but certainly, there will be an abundance!

Jesus, I long for your happiness! I long to be caught up in the beautiful vision of your joy and revelation. Take me, and make me into the faithful servant who longs for your return.

True Superhero

He is your praise and he is your God, who has done for you
these great and awe-inspiring works your eyes have seen.

Fairy tales and superhero epics are resplendent with magic
and miraculous deeds of strength and accomplishment. It's
a world where nothing is impossible. Even mere mortals
who happen into the realm can, if gifted by supreme powers,
achieve legendary feats of their own. Alas, these are only
stories for entertainment. There are no fairy godmothers,
and as much as we would like Superman to come to our
rescue, he won't. But our God is truthfully miraculous
and all-powerful. From creation to the parting of the Red
Sea, from Jesus' birth to his resurrection, he performs the
supernatural regularly. There is only one true superhero, and
his name is Jehovah El-Shaddai—the Lord God Almighty. It
is he who deserves our praise.

*Lord God Almighty, why is it me that you have chosen to
be your son? Why have you selected me from among all the
people of the earth to honor you and belong with you? I
stand in awe.*

Hard Knocks

I have learned the secret of being content
in any and every situation.

PHILIPPIANS 4:11 NIV

Our time on this earth is like a blink of our Father's eye,
and throughout our lives we will witness both poverty and
plenty. The Lord provides as he sees fit and always has a
plan unfolding in the background, despite how it may feel at
times. During times of difficulty, we must praise the Lord for
how we are being strengthened to serve him more effectively.
In times of rest and plenty, we shall praise him for his
blessings in our lives and use them for his glory.

*Lord, you have brought me into your presence even while
I stand here on earth. Remind me that these current trials
are here for a purpose. May I learn to depend on you in
abundance and in need.*

Hate Evil

You who love the LORD, hate evil!
He protects the lives of his godly people
and rescues them from the power of the wicked.

PSALM 97:10 NLT

You turn on the news in the morning, or open a newspaper, and every day it's full of the same stories. Atrocities around the world are committed each day. By now, it's become so normal that we are sometimes immune to it. Until it affects our lives directly, we might not even notice it. We are asked to hate evil. We aren't told to merely put up with evil, or to make sure that we don't let it bother us. We are supposed to loathe it. What does that mean for us? It means that we should pray for those who are affected by such evil, and we should look for ways to help. We can offer hope to those who are suffering.

Dear God, I pray for my friends and enemies who are consumed by the evil desires and forces around them. I ask you to shine a light into their dark world and teach them your ways, so they would be able to resist temptation.

So Good

LORD, answer me because your love is so good.
Because of your great kindness, turn to me.
PSALM 69:16 NCV

Think of different scenarios that you have described as being
good. Perhaps it was a delicious home-cooked meal. Maybe
a compelling film, a long hike, a steaming cup of coffee, or a
well-placed conversation. *So good.* These memories should
evoke feelings of warmth and attachment. Can you, do you,
think of God in the same manner? When someone brings
up the things of God, do you think *so good*, or do you cringe
a little? Over time, it is easy to become cynical toward God.
Perhaps our prayers are not answered the way we thought
they should be, suffering comes, or we are hurt by his people.
Search your heart. How could cynicism be stealing your view
of a God whose love is *so good?*

*God, why do I get wrapped up in my own opinions and
pessimism? I wish I could live constantly with hope, resisting
the doubts that rise within me. Lord of all kindness, wash me
clean of my cynicism.*

He Is Worthy

You are worthy, our Lord and God, to receive glory and
honor and power, for you created all things, and by your will
they were created and have their being.

REVELATION 4:11 NIV

No matter what obstacles you are facing today, God is
worthy of your honor and praise. No matter what kind of
troubles you find, he is still the King of glory, reigning over
all. He created all things, and in him, you find your being.
You are at home in him. Come home to his peace today. Lift
high the name of Jesus as you pour your heart out to him in
prayer. He is as worthy today as he was when he resurrected
from the grave. He is unchanging in love, always overflowing
with mercy and grace. Run into his presence, letting his
kindness draw you in. He will never turn you away.

*Creator God, through you and by you all things came into
being. You brought matter out of a void of darkness and
created a world of light. I praise you, Jesus, for redeeming
this world by your blood on the cross.*

He Listens

"Then you will call upon Me and go and pray to Me, and I will listen to you."

JEREMIAH 29:12 NKJV

Have you ever tried to hold a conversation with someone and realized that they have not listened to a word you said? Frustrating, isn't it? You might try to talk louder, or even say something silly, alarming, or nonsensical to get their attention. You can be thankful that God promises when you talk to him, he will listen. You never have to work to get his interest; he is always ready and eager to hear from you. Don't waste this privilege; call on him today.

God, if you are listening, why do I feel so alone? Why do I question my faith in you, and why do doubts arise? Please give me hope in your presence, pushing aside the dark cloud that has taken up residence above me.

Satisfied Hunger

He has satisfied the thirsty
and filled the hungry with good things.

PSALM 107:9 CSB

Our physical hunger, and how we satisfy it, can tell us a
lot about how we can best satisfy the hunger of our soul.
You know that if you skip a meal, you can become overly
emotional or irritated, and it can lead to poor concentration.
If you eat too much, you might become sleepy or ill. Apply
these same principles to your spiritual nourishment:
regularly fill your soul with words from God and don't skip
time with him.

*Precious Lord and Savior, I have so many needs, and the
greatest of them all is my need for your nourishment. Be
near to me and fill me up when I am dry. Remind me each
day of my need for you, and I will not forget.*

Still Praying

He is able to save to the uttermost those who draw near to God through him, since he always lives to make intercession for them.

HEBREWS 7:25 ESV

Some people have the benefit of being prayed for their entire lives. From birth, they have had a steady stream of prayers by faithful family members. That isn't the case for everyone. Do not dismay if this doesn't describe your experience. There is one who has prayed for you from the beginning. His name is Jesus. It is his delight, and a sign of his inheritance for you, that he prays. He sits right beside his Dad, with scarred hands, asking for the reality of the completed work on the cross to become your daily victory.

Jesus, please intercede on my behalf, for I fail in all too many ways. I draw near to you this day and pray that you would save me from the weight of my sin and mistakes. What can I do without you?

Love not Sacrifice

"I want you to show love, not offer sacrifices.
I want you to know me more than I want burnt offerings."

HOSEA 6:6 NLT

If someone said they loved you— even brought you flowers every day—but never made time for you or ever really talked to you, would you truly feel loved by them? How connected can you feel to someone you're never actually connecting with? Since God is the author of love, why would we expect him to feel any differently? He loves it when we profess our love for him. He loves it when we sacrifice our time and money for the things he cares about. But he feels most loved by us when we reach out to connect with him. Pray, journal, sing, or get into his creation and quietly ponder. How we connect isn't important. He wants to know us, and he wants us to know him.

God, I apologize today for all the ways I have offered lip service and paid my dues to your name while not cultivating a relationship with you. Please show me that building a relationship with you is more important than anything else in this world.

Lovely before Him

Hallelujah! Praise the Lord!
How beautiful it is when we sing
our praises to the beautiful God;
for praise makes you lovely before him
and brings him great delight!
He heals the wounds of every shattered heart.

PSALM 147:1, 3 TPT

Whether you are carrying pain and suffering from past abuse or tragedy, or you've more recently been hurt, run toward the one who heals. There is no requirement or need too great; God will piece you back together. It might take some work. It will take constant communion with him to remind you of his healing power, but he will glue you back until you are whole. Broken souls, broken bodies, be reminded of his power in these moments and do not turn away.

I am joyful, Lord, to know that my praises are your delight! Though I am just a speck in the universe, my exaltation rises to you as a fragrant source of happiness. May my praises be pleasing in your sight today.

Healing through Jesus

Jesus was going about in all of Galilee, teaching in their synagogues and proclaiming the gospel of the kingdom, and healing every disease and every sickness among the people.

MATTHEW 4:23 NASB

It is hard to understand how and when God heals his children. Have you prayed for healing recently and haven't got any better? Do you know someone around you that is unwell and not recovering? It can be disheartening when sickness lingers. Our faith does not need to be great, but through our belief in Jesus, we can also acknowledge our belief in the miracles that he performed. Jesus showed us that what we think is impossible is possible with God.

God, nothing is possible by my might. I am without ability apart from you, so breathe your power into me and make me the vessel of your change. I pray today that I would be a source of healing for those around me.

Hear and Protect

Bend down, O LORD, and hear my prayer;
answer me, for I need your help.

PSALM 86:1 NLT

In this world full of independence, we have not had to practice the art of asking for help. None of us want to impose ourselves on anyone; we don't want to make a fuss, and we think we should be able to do things on our own. But God didn't create you to be on your own or have to do things by yourself. Today, ask him for answers, ask him for help, ask him for protection and trust that he will save you.

God, I desire answers for the questions that fill my mind. I need help for the trials that litter my path. Yet in all this, give me virtue to meet the day. Give me patience for my questions, strength for my trials, and trust in your plan.

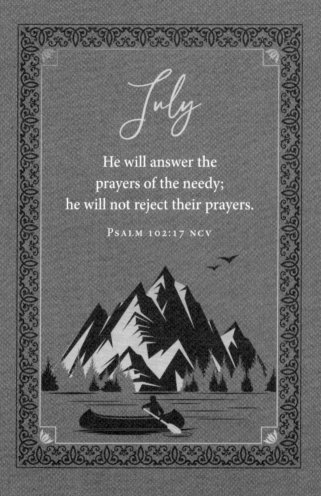

July

He will answer the
prayers of the needy;
he will not reject their prayers.

PSALM 102:17 NCV

My Cry

LORD, hear my prayer,
listen to my cry for mercy;
in your faithfulness and righteousness
come to my relief.

PSALM 143:1 NIV

Do you think David needed to ask the Lord to hear his prayer? This kind of plea resonates with our humanness; it assures us that it's okay to feel like you need to get God's attention. But even in David's request, he establishes the Lord's faithfulness and righteousness. Our prayers and petitions go hand in hand with our humble recognition that our human condition can only be met by a faithful and righteous God. If you are struggling with understanding a situation, or you're trying to adjust to change or impending decisions, allow yourself to surrender to God's mercy. This is the only thing that will bring you peace.

In a blink, you can shine your light on my life, God. You can wash my heart in relief and change my cry for mercy to a battle cry. Hear me and give hope to the hopeless situations which rise to meet me.

Prayers Heard

"If my people, who are called by my name, will humble themselves and pray and seek my face and turn from their wicked ways, then I will hear from heaven, and I will forgive their sin and will heal their land."

2 CHRONICLES 7:14 NIV

Cause and effect may be the earliest concept we grasp. Babies cry, and someone comes to soothe them. Toddlers see different results when they ask politely or throw a tantrum. We sometimes approach prayer from this simple mindset. If I cry out to God, he'll come running. If I ask nicely, he'll give me what I want. However, that's not how prayer works. If we want to be heard, we need to come humbly, quietly, and seek his face. The first step is simply to be in his presence, then we regret that which distances us from him, reject our sins, and ask for forgiveness. Then we can await his response.

Jesus, please cause a change in me, so I would desire what you desire and hate what you hate. I pray for humility where I am proud, weakness where I consider myself strong, and forgiveness for my many sins.

Stilled Storm

Then they cried to the LORD in their trouble,
and he delivered them from their distress.
He made the storm be still,
and the waves of the sea were hushed.

PSALM 107:28-29 ESV

When we face trouble, our immediate reaction is to fix the problem. We are geared toward solving issues. However, we are powerless to solve some problems that we face and find ourselves defeated. But we aren't. We can go boldly to God with our needs and requests, and he will hear us. No problem is bigger than he is, and he doesn't consider our requests insignificant. He deeply cares for each of us, and he will calm raging waters for us.

My issues feel so much bigger than me, loving Lord, but I have heard they are nothing in comparison to your goodness. I pray you would lead me in the fight against my battles and make the storm around me still.

Better than Fireworks

Trust in the LORD and do good.
Then you will live safely in the land and prosper.
Take delight in the LORD,
and he will give you your heart's desires.

PSALM 37:3-4 NLT

The Fourth of July is a time to celebrate America with cookouts and fireworks. It's also a good time for us to think about our blessings as a country. Sometimes we forget to thank God for his blessings of freedom—the opportunity to serve him without fear, to live safely in our country, to prosper financially, and countless other freedoms that we take for granted. On this holiday, we can express our delight in God and thank him for his blessings—especially our freedom to worship him freely.

God, thank you for the safety I enjoy and for the freedom I have to read your Word and worship you. I pray that this right of mine would not go to waste, but that I would use it to spread your name and make you famous.

Heart Motives

"Be careful! When you do good things, don't do them in front of people to be seen by them. If you do that, you will have no reward from your Father in heaven."

MATTHEW 6:1 NCV

The good works we do are the evidence that our faith is alive. Good deeds are a vital aspect of our lives as believers. The average person living in biblical times would have considered the Pharisees to be exemplary in their righteous living. However, the Pharisees were also known for making a show of their good deeds. This admonition from Jesus reaches the level of our hearts, testing our motivations for why we perform acts of kindness. If we believe that our righteousness rests on Christ, we won't need to seek the approval of other people. God working in us grants us the strength to do good. In view of his grace toward us, our deeds become a spontaneous outpouring of praise.

God, my heart and mind are deceptive. I cannot become righteous by my own strength. I pray that you would make a change in my heart that goes beyond my ability and displays yours.

Enlightened with Hope

I pray that the eyes of your heart may be enlightened, so that
you will know what is the hope of His calling, what are the
riches of the glory of His inheritance in the saints.

EPHESIANS 1:18 NASB

When we believe and hope for the best for those around
us, we carry our faith into our relationships. There is a
greater hope waiting for each of us in the kingdom of Christ.
Though we walk through trials and storms of many kinds,
they are not indicators of our place in God's kingdom. When
our friends cannot see the way out of the dark, we can stand
with them and keep watch. Let's pray for their comfort, their
peace, their understanding, and their breakthrough. What
are friends for if not to hold each other up when we cannot
stand on our own?

*God, I pray over my friends who are walking in hardship
and darkness. I pray for their comfort, their peace, and
above all for their relationship with you. Please draw them
closer to you through their trials; enlighten their hearts and
give them hope.*

Heart's Posture

Oh, that I might have my request,
and that God would fulfill my hope.

JOB 6:8 ESV

Did Job get it? You know, the one request that he wanted to have fulfilled. Look around at the context: do we even get to know what that one request was? Perhaps the bigger question is, does it really matter? What matters is the posture of Job's heart toward God. In light of eternity, maybe it's not the subject of our prayers that holds the most significance but the posture of our hearts. Do we turn to God in prayer, cry out to him, or have a heart of submission to his will? First and foremost, God wants us to come to him in prayer with hearts that say, "Your will be done."

God, please give me a posture of reverence and love. May my relationship with you be founded on righteousness and understanding not fear or pride. I have many requests, but I pray that you would teach me to present them all humbly to you.

Heavenly Comfort

Wait for the LORD's help.
Be strong and brave,
and wait for the LORD's help.

PSALM 27:14 NCV

As children, we sought out our mother or father for comfort when we were hurt. A hug, soft words, a bandage, or a kiss brought comfort and contentment. The pain might have still been there, but we felt secure and loved. What a wonderful feeling that was. Where do we go when we are hurt, afraid, or stressed now? What do we do when we feel unsure, mentally beat down, or anxious? It really is true that "a burden shared is a burden halved." We can share our hurts with the Lord. God has promised to help us shoulder our problems.

God, please be my security and love. Be my comfort in grief, my strength in weakness, and my companion in loneliness. I have you at all times to rely on and trust in. My heart will be secure in the knowledge of your salvation.

Help Guaranteed

I asked the LORD for help, and he answered me.
He saved me from all that I feared.

PSALM 34:4 NCV

Do you ever get so caught up in your fear that you feel
you are panicking to find a way to eliminate it? You think
of various scenarios for controlling what seems to be
uncontrollable. You seek advice from people who claim to
have the answers you are seeking, but none of them help.
And then a lightbulb comes on, and you consider prayer. We
would all save a lot of time and heartache if we would believe
the psalmist's testimony that God hears when we ask for
help, and he answers. When doubt comes, don't waste time;
go to the only one who can listen and solve your deepest
despair.

*There is so much that I am afraid of, Lord. I have doubts, I
have addictions, and I have a multitude of spiritual trials
pressing in on me. But you are the God of faith, and I trust
in you. I trust you.*

Highways to Zion

Blessed is the person whose strength is in You,
In whose heart are the roads to Zion!

PSALM 84:5 NASB

The ancient Hebraic form of writing often presented literal and figurative pictures side by side. Zion, or Jerusalem, is where the temple of God stood. People walked a long highway to get there, so desperate were they to be in the presence of God. David recognized that true strength is cultivated through a loving relationship with God and a heart bent on being in God's presence. We no longer have to travel to a distant temple to go before the Lord, for we have the Spirit of God living within us.

Spirit of the Living God, dwell richly in me! Let your light shine through every part of my being and your strength occupy my whole soul. Without you, I am lost and afraid. Come to me and make me your dwelling place.

Mercy Endures

Oh, give thanks to the LORD, for He is good!
For His mercy endures forever.

1 CHRONICLES 16:34 NKJV

God's mercy never runs out. He doesn't get fed up with you
when you sin and say, "Well that's it! I'm done with you!" His
mercy endures. It goes on and on past all you could imagine.
When you love the Lord, you don't want to sin, but you are
right in the middle of the journey of sanctification. Don't let
shame and condemnation whisper the lies that his mercy has
run out on you. His mercy endures forever. Give thanks for
this wonderful news!

*God, surely you are infinite in all you do! Your grace knows
no bound, your mercy no end. Help me to trust in you like
I have trusted in no one before. Precious Savior, if I cannot
trust in your enduring mercy I am without help.*

Mighty Works

Praise him for his mighty works;
praise his unequaled greatness!

PSALM 150:2 NLT

Can you remember a time when you were astounded by an answer to prayer? Has there ever been a moment in your life that had no earthly explanation? God is a God of miracles. He restores what was stolen, and he redeems what seemed lost forever. In his earthly ministry, Jesus healed the sick, drove out tormenting spirits, and raised the dead. He still does these things today. He is the God who defends the vulnerable, who reaches beyond the boundaries of religion, and who loves perfectly and powerfully.

God, you are the picture of all things good. You stand up for those no one else notices. You love the unloved and fight the greatest adversaries with ease. You are a God of both strength and humility, and I praise you for this.

Humble Servant

He poured water into a basin.
Then he began to wash the disciples' feet,
drying them with the towel he had around him.

JOHN 13:5 NLT

When was the last time you prayed for humility? God wants you to walk in humility because it is the kingdom way, and anything that is the kingdom way is the best way. He doesn't want to punish you. He wants the best for you. He wants to make you like Christ to refine you. Don't fall into the trap of not praying for kingdom traits because you are afraid you will get hard situations. Pray for humility, so God can refine you and make you more like him.

Lord Jesus, if I only had half the humility you showed to your disciples, I would be well beyond where I am now. I am proud, and I have a hardened heart. Please wash my feet, humble me, and recreate my poor heart.

Boast in Weakness

If I must boast,
I will boast of the things that show my weakness

2 CORINTHIANS 11:30 NIV

"You did an incredible job; you're so talented!" How do you respond? Going beyond "thank you" and actually accepting—embracing—the kind words being spoken about us is difficult for many. We may have been told it's rude not to say "thank you" when complimented, but society also sends an opposing message: we'd best not be perceived as agreeing. No one wants to be labeled vain. So how freeing is it to learn that everything good about us is actually about Jesus? Every good gift, from beauty to a lovely singing voice to the ability to sink a three-pointer on the basketball court or nail a presentation in front of important clients, is from him. You're not full of yourself; you're full of him! Brag about his awesomeness.

Precious Savior, you are my boast! You are my strength in the battle and my humility in the stray moments. I glorify you, for you are my every good thing! Without you I am an empty shell without virtue or purpose.

Hurled into the Sea

"You hurled me into the depths, into the very heart of the seas, and the currents swirled about me; all your waves and breakers swept over me. I said, 'I have been banished from your sight; yet I will look again toward your holy temple.'"

JONAH 2:3-4 NIV

It doesn't matter whether you feel like you are drowning because you have intentionally walked away from God or whether circumstances have simply overwhelmed you. Expressing how you feel about being distant from God is important. If you feel like this today, tell God. In the same way that you express your sorrow, be intentional about directing your words and heart toward him. Look to his holy temple, not away from it. God is near and will answer your cries.

God, why do I cry out? It feels hopeless, but surely the darkness does not last forever. Surely the sea has a coast, and you are the port in every storm. Give me faith, for I am worn thin by the life behind me.

I Will Praise

I will hope continually
and will praise you more and more.

PSALM 71:14 CSB

Our hope is not in the mountains or valleys in which we
tread. It is not found in the circumstances of our lives.
Our anticipation lies in the working out of God's faithful
character. He who is slow to anger, abounding in love, who
makes all things new in his mercy, he is our great confidence.
When our hearts begin to waver, may they be strengthened
by his nearness.

*I will not dismay, Lord. I will not be shaken by the attacks of
the enemy, for my feet are on solid ground. You are my shield
and the object of my every request and praise.*

Meet with Him

Draw near to God,
and he will draw near to you.

JAMES 4:8 ESV

God is so pleased when we stop to be with him. When
we set time apart just to seek him, read his Word, pray,
and bring him honor, he comes to meet us. He is with us
throughout our day and is interested in every aspect of our
lives, but when he sees us stop and look for him it brings
him satisfaction. This verse is a promise: when you come to
meet the Lord, he comes to meet with you. The more time
you spend with him, the easier it becomes to hear him speak.
Take some time to be with him today!

*God, I pray that you would provide for me a time to draw
near to you in prayer and meditation today. I pray that you
would open my heart to your Word and let it speak to me
today.*

Call on Him

Hear my prayer, LORD; listen to my cry for mercy.
When I am in distress, I call to you, because you answer me.
PSALM 86:7 NIV

All too often we can find ourselves, in our very full and busy lives, utterly alone. We feel misunderstood, an outcast of our doing. We isolate ourselves in a world of pain, feeling as though there is no one to whom we can turn. There is good news! There is someone who always answers when we call. God is waiting for us to call on him. He has enough love to go around—enough for anybody willing to seek it out. When we cry for mercy, he hears our cries.

Savior and Friend, please speak to me today. Answer me from heaven, for I am in distress without your presence. I need you so desperately. May my conversation and prayer to you continue throughout today.

I Wish

He satisfies your desires with good things
so that your youth is renewed like the eagle's.

PSALM 103:5 NIV

I wish I may, I wish I might
Have the wish I wish tonight.
I wish…
When you're soaping up in the shower or staring out the
window at the moon, what do you secretly wish for? To be tall
or funny or really good at something? To have a best friend
or a home of your own? Everything you long for is something
that God sees and knows. You don't have to tell him what
you wish for; he already knows. But he likes it when you tell
him just the same. God isn't a make-a-wish kind of God. He
doesn't wave a magic wand over us and give us three wishes.
But he does care, and he does answer prayer—not always in
the way we expect, but in a way that satisfies.

Thank you, Father, for caring deeply about me. Thank
you for knowing my every desire and every need and
understanding the right time for their satisfaction. I entrust
my life to your plan today and pray that you would be at
work in a mighty way.

Immeasurably More

To him who is able to do immeasurably more than all we ask or imagine, according to his power that is at work within us, to him be glory...for ever and ever! Amen.

EPHESIANS 3:20-21 NIV

In the midst of trial and change, when requests are ever on our minds, it can feel like we are running out God's patience. We continually ask for the overwhelming needs in our lives to be met. God is full of patience, and he delights in us whenever we come to him. When we live in a posture of open relationship with him, both giving and receiving, we find that he is abundantly better than our wildest hopes. It doesn't matter how many times you've asked—bring your requests to God. He never tires of your voice. As you pour out your heart to him, take some time to receive his perspective and love for you.

Lord Jesus, I come to you again with requests and complaints. Thank you for never growing tired of my requests nor of my voice as I cry out to you. I pray that I would remain in humility and reverence as I go through my day.

In His Name

"If you ask me anything in my name,
I will do it."

JOHN 14:14 CSB

What is in a name? In our modern world, names don't carry as much weight as they used to. Back in the days of Jesus and John, your name was also your rank and your placeholder. In many cultures, it qualified you and proved your status. Looking back on history, many a decree or law was carried out in the name of the king, emperor, or presiding ruler. That name carried authority and power, and it was law as far as the ruler's territory extended. Even the most powerful human names can't compare to the name of Jesus. His name holds power in every situation.

Your name is power over darkness, Jesus. Your name is the banner I raise when Satan raises his attack against me. When there is noise all around me, your name cuts through it with majesty and greatness.

My God

LORD, you are my God;
I will exalt you and praise your name,
for in perfect faithfulness you have done wonderful things,
things planned long ago.

ISAIAH 25:1 NIV

If the Lord is truly our God, then our lives will show it. With loving trust and humble surrender, we will live out his mercy in little and big ways. We will not seek to promote ourselves at the expense of others. We won't look for ways to demean people when we have the chance to lift them up. May our lives, hearts, and words line up in the truth of who we are and who we serve.

Lord God, I pray that I would live a life worthy of your calling. I pray that you would truly be my God, not just in word but in truth. May you be active in my life, and may it be evident to those around me.

In the Secret

"When you pray, do not be like the hypocrites, for they love to pray standing in the synagogues and on the street corners to be seen by others. Truly I tell you, they have received their reward in full. But when you pray, go into your room, close the door and pray to your Father, who is unseen. Then your Father, who sees what is done in secret, will reward you"

MATTHEW 6:5-6 NIV

Cherish the secret things. So much of our life is for others. Whether it is the requirement of jobs, keeping up relationships, or the programs we volunteer for, so much of our time and energy is spent on other people. God wants our time. He wants it for us and for him. Maybe this will require a designated prayer closet or a quiet place away. Maybe we head outside with our Bible and journal to sneak away for a while. However we do it, our heavenly Father sees us. What a faithful gift that thought alone is; he sees us in secret and will meet us where we are.

I love the close relationship I have with you, God. I pray that I would have time today to draw near to you in prayer and to present my day's troubles and emotions. Please be at work, and please hear my quiet prayer.

The Valleys

I trust in your unfailing love;
my heart rejoices in your salvation.
I will sing the LORD's praise,
for he has been good to me.

PSALM 13:5-6 NIV

Do you have something in your life that has felt like a consistent battle? Have you felt the heaviness of sorrow settle in like a fog? If you are feeling consistently defeated, know that even then you can trust the Lord. His love is unfailing. Remember that you can praise him for what he has already done. Bolster your faith by remembering his good works. Bring your heart, whole or broken, to the Lord and remember that his unfailing love is what sustains you.

God, I pray that you would help me to recall your many good works for me. Remind me of what you are capable of and that my circumstances are nothing in comparison to your power.

Lovely for You

This is my prayer for you: that your love will grow more and more; that you will have knowledge and understanding with your love; that you will see the difference between good and bad and will choose the good; that you will be pure and without wrong for the coming of Christ.

PHILIPPIANS 1:9-10 NCV

What if, as members of God's holy Church, we made this our prayer for one another? What if each morning we prayed this over one another? Instead of competing ideologies and cooler buildings and more entertaining social media feeds, what if we prayed that each and every place the gospel is adopted and shared would see this beautiful blessing? Ask God for this today.

Jesus, I pray that you would strengthen my church in love. Be at work in it, changing it and shaping it into your image. Help us not to let our differences defeat our unity.

Brave Belief

"Truly, truly, I say to you, whoever believes in me will also do the works that I do; and greater works than these will he do, because I am going to the Father. Whatever you ask in my name, this I will do, that the Father may be glorified in the Son."

JOHN 14:12-13 NLT

One of the bravest, most courageous things we can do as children of God is simply to believe him at his word. He takes great delight when his children trust that all his promises are good and true. Today, refuse cynicism, skepticism, and arrogance and instead courageously say to the Father, "I will trust you, and by faith, ask great things in your name."

I pray, Holy Spirit, that you would be alive in me today. In the strength of your power, make me a vessel of the change you want to see in this world.

Incredible

The LORD merely spoke,
and the heavens were created.
He breathed the word,
and all the stars were born.

PSALM 33:6 NLT

Stop for a minute and listen to the sounds around you. Have you ever studied how the ear works? Sounds make vibrations in the air that are captured by the shape of the outer ear and canal. These sound waves cause the eardrum to vibrate which sets three miniscule bones and then fluid into motion. Tiny hair cells bend turning that into electrical signals. These signals are sent along our auditory nerve to our brain where we interpret sound. *Incredible.* It is important, even necessary, for mankind to pause and take time to consider what God has made. When we do, we begin to realize how incredibly worthy of praise he is.

As I stare into the heavens, there is no shortage of miracles for me to stand in awe of. You are beyond all description in your greatness, Creator God, and I am unable to fathom the love you have for me.

Incredible God

The heavens tell of the glory of God;
And their expanse declares the work of His hands.
Day to day pours forth speech,
And night to night reveals knowledge.

PSALM 19:1-2 NASB

If you desire a transformed life, learn to be a person who lives in awe of God. Awe and wonder are qualities often missing from our modern lives. Search engines, just a tap away, provide all the answers we need. Social media and TV pour the headlines into us constantly, and even GPS systems leave no room for wandering. We listen intently to all these sources, but when was the last time we took a moment to listen to what was being said in nature? God is revealed through the heavens and the works of his hands. He is endless and wonderful, and our lives are transformed when we stop and listen to the praise of his glory.

God, I pray today that my problems and worries would be overshadowed by your glory. When things are tough and life gets hard, remind me that you remain great in your power and compassion.

Intimate Companion

"God is spirit, and those who worship him
must worship in spirit and truth."

JOHN 4:24 ESV

How do you define spirit? An athlete triumphing over great
hardship is said to have an indomitable spirit. A feisty,
strong-willed child is sometimes described as spirited.
What's being described in both cases is something beyond
the body, something intangible. Though equally intangible,
the Holy Spirit exists for us to discover. He works in our lives
by teaching, comforting, and protecting us. His promptings
tell us when to move closer and when to pull back. The Spirit
is our intimate companion and wholly deserving of our
worship.

*Holy Spirit, I pray for you to be working in me a new way
today. Please take the struggles I have been facing for so long
and renew my strength to conquer them. Make me a vessel of
your change.*

It Matters

"Whoever can be trusted with very little can also be trusted with much, and whoever is dishonest with very little will also be dishonest with much."

LUKE 16:10 NIV

Life cannot be one long mountaintop experience, and it also will not be only a deep, hard valley. There are thousands of moments in between: washing dishes, finishing a work report, checking the mail, taking care of animals, having coffee. Does God care about these moments? Yes, he does, for these are the moments that make up our life. We can build a life that is a monument of praise to our Creator one brick, or one moment, at a time. We can experience God no matter where we are or what we are doing. He doesn't expect constant service from us, but he does desire consistent communion with us.

Lord God, I pray today that you would make me a good steward of the things you have given me. Teach me to be faithful in every trial, whether trivial or monstrous.

It Is Time

Plant the good seeds of righteousness,
and you will harvest a crop of love.
Plow up the hard ground of your hearts,
for now is the time to seek the LORD,
that he may come
and shower righteousness upon you.

HOSEA 10:12 NLT

It seemed like it was too late for Israel. They had been given opportunity after opportunity, and they just kept rebelling against God and not following his ways. They hardened their hearts against him time and time again. But in this beautiful verse, God says there is still time. Even if it is like a late October day, with frost already on the ground, you can still plant, and God will still harvest. He never gives up on us.

God, please teach me to never give up on repentance. You are faithful to forgive me thousands upon thousands of times. Why do I question it? I am sorry for the pride that keeps me from you.

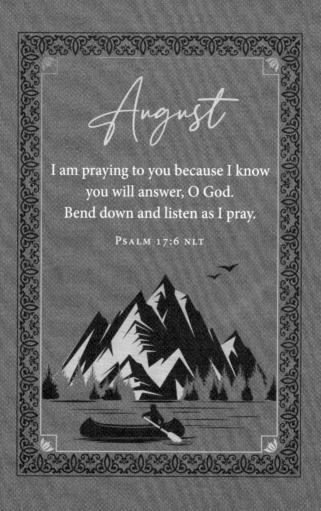

August

I am praying to you because I know
you will answer, O God.
Bend down and listen as I pray.

Psalm 17:6 nlt

Joyful Song

Make a joyful noise to the LORD, all the earth!
Serve the LORD with gladness!
Come into his presence with singing!

PSALM 100:1-2 ESV

Do you ever feel so happy, you just want to sing? Singing is one of the ways we can express to God how much we love him. There's nothing like the joy that knowing the Lord brings us, and it only makes sense that his love would make us want to sing his praise. Worshipping the Lord with song is a concept that has been around for ages. When we come before him with joyful songs, we are joining scores of believers from years past and all of heaven as well. Together we praise him. God loves to hear you sing. Praise him like he deserves to be praised.

How glorious you are, that you saw me, a sinner, and chose to make me your son! Thank you, God, for the love and the gladness with which you have filled my heart. I am yours, and you are mine.

Just Today

> "Our Father in heaven, hallowed be your name. Your kingdom come, your will be done, on earth as it is in heaven. Give us this day our daily bread, and forgive us our debts, as we also have forgiven our debtors. And lead us not into temptation, but deliver us from evil."
>
> MATTHEW 6:9-13 ESV

Today's verses contain what is perhaps the most well-known prayer in the world. Jesus gave it to his disciples when they asked him to teach them to pray. The Lord's Prayer has within it a basic formula of sorts for our daily conversations with God. First, acknowledge and praise God for being God. Next, ask for today's needs to be met, sins forgiven, and temptations resisted. Bring your time before God as a daily act of surrender. The day Jesus wants us to be most focused on, and most surrendered to, is this one.

Lord, my cares and burdens are many, but I lift up today's worries to you. My future will not be improved by my worry. Please give me faith in your providential arm and in your care for me.

Never Give Up

Jesus told his disciples a parable to show them
that they should always pray and not give up.

LUKE 18:1 NIV

When you persist in prayer, it can't be guaranteed that you
will get what you prayed for. There is a guarantee though
that talking to him constantly and asking him tirelessly can
only lead to a deeper and more intimate relationship with
him. Isn't that the ultimate win? Though we do not have
the promise that our persistent prayers will for sure change
things, they will for sure change *us*. Persistent prayer is a win
for you because it brings you closer to Jesus. Don't give up
when things don't go how you planned. Keep praying, keep
seeking, and know that God is faithful.

*Jesus, I will not cease to lift my voice to you in prayer. When
life does not make sense and I am in search of answers, I will
not stop asking you for what I need. Sustain me in prayer so
I am not be discouraged.*

Keep Things Simple

Don't be intimidated by those who are older than you;
simply be the example they need to see by being faithful
and true in all that you do. Speak the truth and live a life of
purity and authentic love as you remain strong in your faith.

1 TIMOTHY 4:12 TPT

This world can feel heavy; sometimes it's good to have a way
to lighten the burden. One of those ways could be to talk to
trusted older friends. Learn from their wisdom. Keep things
simple and always speak the truth. Let God heal your heart.
Think about his steady love in your situation. Thank him for
the younger people in your life and pray to be an example for
them.

*God, make me an example for those around me. I know I
fail and am insufficient in more ways than I can count, yet I
pray that you would still use me. I want to be an example of
your faithful love transforming a simple sinner.*

Keeping Pace

I have fought an excellent fight.
I have finished my full course with all my might
and I've kept my heart full of faith.

2 TIMOTHY 4:7 TPT

When a person first starts training for a marathon, it's a common mistake to take off as fast as possible. But every runner must learn to find a pace that they can set for the whole race. Some playlists have been developed with a specific bpm (beats per minute). This helps a runner align their pace with the music, so they can achieve their goal. In the same fashion, we need to find the rhythm of the Holy Spirit in life and keep pace with him. Trying to race ahead will leave you weary; being complacent will put you behind. Ask the Holy Spirit to align your pace with his today.

Holy Spirit, please bring me into harmony with you. Teach me to listen to your Word, follow your lead, and abide by your ways. I am an empty vessel, so please fill me up and make me whole.

Know for Yourself

It was your own eyes that saw all these
great things the Lord has done.

DEUTERONOMY 11:7 NIV

We read in the Bible about the miracles God did. People like
Moses and Esther and Hannah prayed, and God answered
their prayers in amazing ways. Sometimes you want to know
for yourself that God is great. Experiencing things up close
and seeing with your own eyes can encourage you and make
your faith strong. Be honest with the Lord and ask him to
show you that he is God.

*Truly, you are God Almighty. So often I struggle to see it.
Please, open the eyes of my heart so that I would behold you
in your glory. Let me see the great things you have done and
know that it is you.*

Big and Small

"Let us praise the Lord, the God of Israel, because he has come to help his people and has given them freedom. He has given us a powerful Savior."

LUKE 1:68-69 NCV

From the beginning of time, God had a plan to bring redemption to mankind. He worked through many different people and periods, and in just the right time, Jesus came. Our God is an all-knowing, all-powerful God who is aware of even the smallest details of humanity. He sees and cares about the tiniest details of your life. He is powerful enough to work big miracles and also move in small ways. Won't you praise him for this today?

Lord Jesus, you are a Savior exceeding all others in power and grace. There is not a sinner you cannot redeem, a corrupted heart you cannot change. Your grace strengthens me when I am weak and fills me up when I am dry.

Lacking Wisdom

If any of you lacks wisdom, you should ask God,
who gives generously to all without finding fault,
and it will be given to you.

JAMES 1:5 NIV

It is easy to say we want wisdom and to ask God for it, but when those difficult decisions come and we feel trapped between a rock and a hard place, what we truly rely on becomes evident. Do we trust ourselves first? Would we rather follow the systems of this world? Or is our first response to turn to God's Word and prayer? The Lord promises to supply what we're lacking and give us the answers we need. He does not treat us with disdain for our lack of wisdom but invites us to partake in his.

God, all too often I trust my needs with myself. Please teach
me to turn to you and to seek after your wisdom. Teach me
to have faith when the future is doubtful, depending on you
for my every ounce of strength.

Lavished with Love

See what great love the Father has lavished on us, that we should be called children of God! And that is what we are! The reason the world does not know us is that it did not know him.

1 JOHN 3:1 NIV

You, child of God, are highly valued. Maybe you tend to see God as a king, a ruler, a tyrant, or a boss. It might seem simplistic but remember that he is your kind and gentle Father. His tenderness is in perfect unity with his power and majesty. He is not more one than the other. In your time with him today, climb up on his lap and rest in the safety that is found there. In that space, even if just for a minute, you can take a deep breath and let him love you. He is delighted by your acknowledgement of who he is.

Thank you, God, for loving me with an unconditional love. Thank you for turning my shame into dancing and my sin into white robes of joy. Thank you for making me your son.

Laying Down Dreams

I know you can do all things,
and that no purpose of Yours can be thwarted.

JOB 42:2

What a beautiful thing it is to be living in step with the purposes of God. And not just a god, but the Alpha and the Omega, the all-knowing, all-powerful, only true God of the universe. How can we know that our dreams and plans align with his purposes? Learn to study God's Word for yourself; don't depend only on what others tell you about it. Pray for wisdom and take direction. If you want to be able to hear God's voice, you must obey in the little things. Be willing to lay your dreams down if he asks you to. Labor over your dreams and goals in prayer, constantly laying them at his feet, and then you will know you are walking in his purpose for you.

God, why did you place these dreams in my heart? Why do I long to do great things and have great relationships if it were never meant to be? Surely you have placed these dreams in me for a reason, so I will bring them to you in prayer.

The Rest Will Follow

Believe on the Lord Jesus Christ,
and you will be saved,
you and your household.

ACTS 16:31 NKJV

It is amazing and delightful to consider how highly God values faith. Abraham believed in the Lord and was declared righteous as a result. When you consider God's faithfulness and choose to believe what he tells you, he will move mountains for you. When you trust him to forgive you and lead you for the rest of your life, others close to you will consider choosing him as well.

God, please forgive me. I am a sinner and can do no good apart from you. I am sorry for all the times I have hurt you or turned from your Word. Please create a change in me, and turn me back to your path.

Learn about Me

"Simply join your life with mine.
Learn my ways and you'll discover
that I'm gentle, humble, easy to please.
You will find refreshment and rest in me."

MATTHEW 11:29 TPT

When was the last time you sat down and had a conversation with your Savior? Our prayers are often the kind that ask for help when things get hard, or request healing of someone close. We might know we are heading into a busy day, so we invite the Holy Spirit to walk alongside us. This is all amazing communication with God, but have you considered the part of the conversation when you start to actively listen to what he might be saying to you? God longs to have deep connection with you. The next time you offer up a prayer, find some time to listen to his response.

I will listen to you, Lord. Teach me your ways; show me your gentleness. You are humble beyond all estimation, so please let me lean on you and walk alongside you. Refresh my soul.

Knocking

"Look! I stand at the door and knock. If you hear my voice and open the door, I will come in, and we will share a meal together as friends."

REVELATION 3:20 NLT

Do you know what is interesting about this verse? It's that you have to open the door. Jesus will knock. He might knock many times. But he won't come in until you've opened the door for him. Jesus won't force his way into your heart or your life because he wants to be welcomed in. He is a gentleman; he won't make you love him. He won't force you to follow him. He gives you full freedom to choose. He will come knocking because he wants a relationship with you. But you must make a choice to invite him in.

Father, for too long I have resisted your voice. I keep trying to make my own way in this world, pushing aside the help I need. I cannot keep going unless you carry me.

Let It Go

In your anger do not sin: Do not let the sun go down while
you are still angry, and do not give the devil a foothold.

EPHESIANS 4:26 NIV

At the end of a long day, it can be easy to let irritation get the
best of you. Jesus never condemned feelings of anger, only
the sin that follows. When anger is not diffused, it can lead
to saying or doing the wrong thing. God gives us a strategy
to deal with our anger, and that is to deal with it quickly—
not carry it with us for the rest of the day. God understands
our frustrations. The next time you feel yourself reacting,
send a prayer his way and ask him to deal with the feelings.
Instead of giving the devil an advantage, give it to the Lord
and let him win the battle for you.

*God, I pray against the work of the devil in my life. He has
designed traps for me at every step, and at times I have fallen
for them. Please conquer my anger, vanquish my fear, and
make me more like you every day.*

Wisdom Poured Out

"To those who listen to my teaching, more understanding will be given. But for those who are not listening, even what little understanding they have will be taken away from them."

MARK 4:25 NLT

Imagine a runner who trains for a marathon, completes it, then stops running. After a year has gone by, he remembers how much fun he had on race day—how satisfying it felt to cross the finish line feeling strong and accomplished. He shows up to run the marathon the next year but, several miles in, he realizes she won't make it. To go the distance, you can't just want to run; you need to train. Following Christ is similar. You need to build—and maintain—your base. Read your Bible. Pray for understanding. Put what you learn into practice every day.

God, I pray that I would develop habits that breathe life into my soul. I pray that through these habits, I would learn your character and become more like you. Take me and mold my soul into your image.

Shameless Joy

David danced with all his might before the LORD. He had on a holy linen vest. David and all the Israelites shouted with joy and blew the trumpets as they brought the Ark of the LORD to the city.

2 SAMUEL 6:14-15 NCV

David did not just dance with all his might before the Lord; he did it in what we would consider his underwear. He was completely unashamed; perhaps making a fool of himself because of how overjoyed he was. Have you ever been so excited that you couldn't keep it to yourself, and you didn't care what it looked like? This is the kind of joy David experienced. Rejoicing is best done in the company of others. Let's not overlook the importance of celebrating both small and big wins in life with others.

I will be undignified in my worship, Lord. I will bear my heart on my chest, shouting for joy and praising your name. God, I pray my joy would be contagious and would spread to those around me as they see the love I have for you.

Call for Help

I look up to the hills,
but where does my help come from?
My help comes from the LORD,
who made heaven and earth

PSALM 121:1-2 NCV

Depending on the type of person you are, you may not be very good at asking for help. There are those who like to be the helpers: they do best serving others because they feel capable and useful. Then there are those who gladly accept service any time they are given the opportunity. Neither is better than the other, and both have their positive elements. In different seasons of life, natural helpers may need to be the ones receiving help. Sometimes this is hard to accept, and we have to be careful not to let pride take control. Asking for help is part of being vulnerable: we push everything aside to say, "I can't do this alone." God has put capable people in our lives who love to help, but they won't know we need help until we ask.

Lord, thank you for the people in my life who have kept me going. They are the instruments of your plan. All around me I see your plan, playing out in a thousand beautiful ways. Thank you.

Life's Song

My loving God, the harp in my heart will praise you.
Your faithful heart toward us will be the theme of my song.
Melodies and music will rise to you, the Holy One of Israel.

PSALM 71:22 TPT

Praise is an intrinsic part of life. You hear the roar of a crowd
when their team wins. The audience applauds after a brilliant
play or musical performance. There are cheers at the dining
room table when you win your favorite board game. Families
hoot and holler when graduates walk across a stage and
when newly married couples kiss. We are created to praise.
We praise what we support, value, and love. So why do we
let embarrassment, pride, or lack of understanding rob us of
showing God that he is our number one? Audible praise is a
sign of a healthy inner spiritual life. Try it this morning!

*I pray that you would create in me a heart of thanksgiving
and love. Thank you, God, for the abundance I enjoy. Even
when life is difficult, your Spirit does not leave me but guides
my heart in the paths of life.*

Life's Leader

When you turn to the right or turn to the left,
you will hear his voice behind you to guide you, saying,
"This is the right path; follow it."

ISAIAH 30:21 TPT

The world is a noisy place. Jesus promises to guide and lead us along the way. But how do we know his voice from the others? The more you listen for God's voice, and the more you tune your ear to hear it, the better you will become at picking him out among the noise. Start in the quiet place, in prayer, listening for his voice. That's your training ground for the noisy world. Become familiar with the kind voice of Christ today.

Speak, Lord Jesus. Let your voice become as familiar to me as the sound of the birds in the sky. I might grow deaf and blind with age, but surely your voice will only become louder as the years roll on.

Lifted Up

Humble yourselves under the mighty power of God,
and at the right time he will lift you up in honor.

1 PETER 5:6 NLT

The longing for significance is something intrinsically woven into each of us. The Lord does not reject the exaltation of humans, in fact he often exalts his faithful followers, but it should not be our focus. By serving God with humility and grace, we forego our pursuits of self-glorification and put our effort toward praising God's name. In the most suitable time and in the most appropriate way, God will raise us up if we relinquish that role to him. We were uniquely made for a God-given purpose, and his plan for our lives is so much greater than anything we can conjure up on our own.

God, I might not understand the path you have me on, but I am sure it is your path. It may not be what I expect, but I pray that you would teach me to desire the plan which you have prepared for me.

Limitless Power

> "Whatever you ask in prayer, believing,
> you will receive it all."
>
> MATTHEW 21:22 NASB

This promise was Jesus' way of telling his disciples that if they had faith in God's power, without doubting it, they would no longer be limited to their own abilities. God's power is limitless, and there is nothing we can ask of him that he is unable to do. This doesn't always mean that he will give us what we want. It does mean that if we put all our trust in him, he will take care of us, and our needs will be met.

All my trust is in you, Lord. All my hope is in you. Though tempters come and winds assail me, yet I stand on the rock of salvation and will not be moved. I trust you, and I will follow your lead to the ends of the earth.

Search Me

Search me, God, and know my heart;
Put me to the test and know my anxious thoughts.

PSALM 139:23 NASB

Searching requires looking in every place available to see what is there. Asking God to search your heart means that you are inviting him to know everything that is in it. Vulnerability is hard particularly when we are battling pride or when we want to hide painful feelings or even sin. Try to be a little more comfortable with vulnerability before God today. Right now, it's just you and him. Tell him exactly how you feel and let him show you how he feels. There is nothing better than hearing how much he loves and accepts you.

God, should I ever have a friend whom I know better than I know you? Surely you are closer than a brother and know me more intimately than a spouse. Teach me to know you in this same way.

Listen to Me

Come, children of God, and listen to me.
I'll share the lesson I've learned of fearing the LORD.
PSALM 34:11 TPT

Is there ever a good time to share your faith lessons with friends? We never quite know when we should be gracious and respect people's journey, or when God might be using us to provide someone with some wisdom. If you are feeling caught between knowing when to speak and when not to speak, pray. When you are seeking the guidance of Jesus, his Holy Spirit will be right there with the words or with the silence.

God, please teach me how and when to share your story. Teach me to not be ashamed of the love which I have in you, and how to display it boldly to those around me. I pray that my life would be a testimony of your love.

Look and Find

If you look for me wholeheartedly,
you will find me.
JEREMIAH 29:13 NLT

Have you ever struggled to feel God's presence? We probably feel that way most when something bad happens in our lives. We wonder where God is when we're hurting. Why isn't he fixing it, or at the very least, why he hasn't spoken to us? God doesn't hide himself. He wants to be found. Go to him. Sit and wait in stillness. Read his Word and hear him speaking to you through the pages. Close your eyes, block out the noise of your life, and seek him. You will find him. He will come to you.

Spirit of the Living God, speak to my soul. Let your love come over me and your power fill me up. Renew me fully as I search after you with my whole heart.

Of Good Courage

Be of good courage,
And He shall strengthen your heart,
All you who hope in the LORD.

PSALM 31:24 NKJV

Today is a new day, and a new opportunity, to look to the Lord. What questions do you have? What hopes are rising in your heart? What disappointments can't you shake? Lay them all before him and invite him to speak into the details. Sometimes, God is just waiting for the invitation of our attention to share his wisdom and perspective. Trust him; what you hear him say will always line up with the Scriptures. Do you dare ask him what he is thinking about?

God, who can fathom the depths of your thoughts? Your ways are not like my ways, so please give me courage when things look hopeless. I am struggling, but I know that my future is in your hands.

Relationship Breakdown

Even my best friend,
the one I trusted completely,
the one who shared my food,
has turned against me.

PSALM 41:9 NLT

Part of becoming close to people is having meals together. A lot can be shared over the dinner table or even a cup of coffee. There is intimacy in opening up your home. Think of someone you feel comfortable doing this with. Often they are the people who are closest to you. Now think of the pain of having these close people turn against you. Our lives involve relationship breakdowns, and when these happen, we need Jesus to intervene. If you are grieving a friendship today, bring it to the Lord in prayer.

What a friend I have in you, Jesus. I pray over the friendships in my life, both for those who have stayed and for those who have left me. Please bless them all with your presence, redeeming their lives in beautiful ways.

Lost

In all your ways submit to him,
and he will make your paths straight.

PROVERBS 3:6 NIV

Have you ever felt lost? You may not know where you are, but God always does. Even if you don't know your way around the world you live in, you only have to ask, and God will give you directions to find your way. Isn't it comforting that he knows where you are and that he can tell you how to get back on the straight path if you just ask him?

God, the path to life is only planned by you. I submit to you my life, my goals, and my dreams. In return, I pray that the crooked path before me would become a straight journey to your throne.

Joy Will Follow

Oh, satisfy us early with Your mercy,
that we may rejoice and be glad all our days!

PSALM 90:14 NKJV

Good news and bad news. Which do you prefer to hear first? Most of us choose the bad news, so we can get it over with. We want to deal with the negative, then move on to happier matters. The New King James translation of Psalm 90:14 offers a similar perspective. By pleading early for mercy, we can turn our attention to the praise, rejoicing, and gladness of life with our God. By handing him our burdens first thing, we are unencumbered when it's time to dance. Seek him first each day, and joy will follow.

God, I give you the day ahead of me. Please satisfy me with your mercy, so I can meet every hardship with joy and faith. There is all too much to accomplish with too little time, but I will rejoice in you all the same.

Love Wins

In return for my love they accuse me,
but I give myself to prayer.
PSALM 109:4 ESV

The ways of the world are different than the ways of the kingdom of God. Jesus made this clear by contrasting what the world says to do with your enemies and what Christ-followers should do. You probably have people in your mind that you see as a threat, or those who are unkind toward you. Sometimes we even get mocked for our faith, whether overtly or subtly. These are the very people Christ asks us to love. It's not easy to pray for those who have hurt you. Jesus understands this; he forgave all who brought him to his painful death on the cross. Allow him to be your strength as you practice goodness to those who have wronged you.

No matter the mockery that faces me, I pray your grace would sustain me. When I am beaten down for what I believe, Lord, may I turn to prayer rather than anger. You have said that the wicked will fall into their own traps.

Intercession

We constantly pray for you, that our God may make you worthy of his calling, and that by his power he may bring to fruition your every desire for goodness and your every deed prompted by faith.

2 THESSALONIANS 1:11 NIV

Do you have someone in life who often tells you they are praying for you? Maybe a parent, a sibling, or a close friend? What a gift they are! Since they have a heart to see you thrive, why not help them by sharing your God-given dreams with them? We know the Lord answers the prayers of the faithful, so, as we invite others to pray for us, we can be confident he will hear them. Our desire to find and fulfill our purpose, our longing to be worthy of the great love of Christ, and the acts we perform in obedience to his calling: all will be blessed by their loving intercession.

God, I pray over someone very important to me today. I pray over their struggles, over their pain, and over everything they have been going through. Please let them know today that you love them.

Mail Joy

When the people heard the letter read out loud, they were
overjoyed and delighted by its encouraging message.

ACTS 15:31 TPT

Letters were the most common long-distance
communication in Bible times. People could be waiting
months or even years before hearing anything from
loved ones. When the church received letters from the
apostles, they were delighted to be encouraged from far
away, knowing they were being prayed for every day. Be
encouraged that others are thinking and praying for you
even though you might not have received that message yet.
In the same way, be thoughtful about others and send a
prayer their way.

*Lord, I pray over those who have no encouragement or joy
today. I pray over the marginalized, the abused, and the
hated. I pray your grace over them, that they would know
the good will you have toward them.*

September

"Keep watch and pray, so that you
will not give in to temptation.
For the spirit is willing,
but the body is weak!"

MATTHEW 26:41 NLT

Hurry

Hurry to help me,
Lord, my salvation!

PSALM 38:22 NASB

When we are in a rush or feeling pressured, sometimes the only thing we can speak, or maybe even think is *Help*. This might be the first time you have stopped for a few minutes in an otherwise rushed day. God doesn't need you to come up with lengthy prayers to explain where you are. If you just feel like you need some help, ask him! The cry in this Scripture is for God to help quickly, and we are allowed to ask him for that. He's here with you right now, ready to save you.

God, deliver me from this tribulation! Let your grace renew my strength, and by your power level the mountain ahead of me. Without you I have no strength, so I cry out to you with all I am.

Make It Happen

> As soon as the people were fed, Jesus told his disciples to get into their boat and to go to the other side of the lake while he stayed behind to dismiss the people.
>
> MATTHEW 14:22 TPT

Burdened and overwhelmed by life, we sometimes need to make time alone happen. Intentional carved-out time for solitude takes wisdom and determination. Jesus, on a short life mission with the greatest purpose in the history of humankind, took time away from his busy schedule. It didn't just happen without deliberate action. Jesus knew the boundaries in his life and can give us wisdom in understanding ours. Perhaps this is a time when you must decide to make time for rest and re-connection with the Father. Make it a matter of intentional prayer. Find solitude and make it happen.

Lord, help me understand that I do not have to do everything. Help me to see that it is not by my power that I conquer my demons, but it is by yours. I trust you. Please give me rest.

Marvelous

Sing to him, sing praise to him;
tell of all his wonderful acts.

1 CHRONICLES 16:9 NIV

Picture the brilliant dawning of a new morning, the sun slowly rising with its radiant glory and bringing another day of life to the world. That is something to celebrate. A sunset, wild with color that paints the sky with vivid expression, is powerful to behold. Sitting under the stars, pointing out the shining spectacle of the Milky Way and each shooting star is a moment of wonder. The works of the Lord are marvelous! Praise him for them today.

God, surely you are marvelous beyond comparison! I see the stars in the sky, the blades of grass in a thousand fields, and know that you have them numbered. Your glory knows no bound, and your greatness no end.

Moment of Solitude

Simon and those who were with Him searched for Him.
When they found Him, they said to Him,
"Everyone is looking for You."

MARK 1:36-37 NKJV

Does this sound like you as you try to step away from the
busyness of the day? Are people looking for you, pressing in
on your alone time? Instead of trying to fit prayer into your
busy day, pray before it gets busy, so you can cope with the
pressures of life. Can you give God some time in the early
morning? Will you find a solitary place to hear from him?
Fight for your time now. Be like Jesus and find the time and
space to wait upon the Father.

*God, help me to find some time in my day to give to you.
May it be a fragrant offering, and a time of relationship in
which I grow closer to you. Refresh me, sustain me, and show
me that you hold my heart in your hand.*

Mountaintops

Your favor, O LORD, made me as secure as a mountain.
Then you turned away from me, and I was shattered.

PSALM 30:7 NLT

It is part of life to have good and bad moments. Sometimes
the hard moments make the good ones seem all the better,
and the good moments make the harder ones feel worse!
You are not alone in the seasonal high and lows of life, so
take some time to think about others around you who might
be going through the same thing. Pray for their situation.
Perhaps they think that God has turned away from them
and they are feeling shattered. You can be an encouragement
simply through your prayers and by letting them know they
are not alone.

*God, your favor seems to have fled from me. It feels like
you have abandoned me, yet I know that you are with me.
I know that in the valley when I feel alone, somehow your
presence follows me even there.*

Music for the Soul

Let us come before him with thanksgiving
and extol him with music and song.

PSALM 95:2 NIV

When was the last time you gave yourself over fully to a time
of worship? Not just singing along to the words in church,
not just bowing your head in prayer, but letting yourself be
completely consumed by the presence of the Lord? Music
is such a gift, and it is little wonder that we want to express
ourselves in a way that reflects the Creator of music! Take
some quiet time today to listen to music and allow God's
divine presence to wash over you, filling every crevice
of your being. Revel in the time that you have with him,
worshiping him in whatever way feels natural to you.

*I worship you, Lord in heaven, for you are worthy of my
adoration. You are worthy of my every honor, worthy of my
every accolade. Your mercy and compassion have renewed
me and changed my corruption to eternal glory.*

Creative Expression

Be filled with the Spirit, speaking to one another with
Psalms, hymns, and songs from the Spirit. Sing and make
music from your heart to the Lord.

EPHESIANS 5:18-19 NIV

Memory is a fascinating part of our brains. We have
memories triggered by sight, smell, and taste. Many
memories are activated by sound. Specific songs can make
or break a moment and stick in your head with relentless
tenacity. As powerful as music is, we often shy away from
using it as a tool. God wants us to participate in musical
expression. Maybe he is nudging you to spend your
commute time listening to worship instead of talk radio.
Don't shy away from expressing yourself in music from your
heart. Fill your life with songs that point your eyes upward
and stir your heart to pray.

*My heart is not always open and willing to sing, God. I pray
that you would fill me with your Spirit and show me how
to express myself with melody and harmony, free from the
worry of looking foolish.*

Holy Helper

"When the Father sends the Spirit of Holiness, the One like me who sets you free, he will teach you all things in my name. And he will inspire you to remember every word that I've told you."

JOHN 14:26 TPT

Facing the Bible can be a daunting task. We don't have to attend Bible college to know the Scriptures well. We don't need a theology teacher or even a pastor to open up the Scriptures and understand God. We have the best teacher of all in the Holy Spirit. In your personal time with God, the Holy Spirit is extremely qualified to teach you about the Word. If you are ever confused about a passage, first turn to him for help. After all, he dwells inside you! Start your Scripture reading time in prayer. You'll be surprised at what you can learn when you submit your daily reading to the Holy Spirit.

Jesus, you promised me your Spirit of Holiness, so I pray today that you would anoint my times of devotion with such a spirit. Give me humility and give me a heart open to your truth.

My Praise

Heal me, LORD, and I will be healed;
Save me and I will be saved,
For You are my praise.

JEREMIAH 17:14 NASB

When we take time to think about how God has met us in life—how he has transformed and built us up in his love—our hearts open up to new possibilities of his goodness. He will always be worthy of praise. He will never fail to follow through on his promises. He is faithful, he is just, he is true, and he works all things together for our good. Whatever we need today, he can provide. Let us lay out all our questions, our hesitations, and our fears before him.

God, I just want to open up my heart and let the contents spill out. I want to give you the fears, the dreams, the realities, and the delusions. Please take me and change me. Help me to have a sense of belonging in you.

Needs Met

The LORD is my strength and my shield;
my heart trusts in him, and I am helped.
Therefore my heart celebrates,
And I will give thanks to him with my song.

PSALM 28:7 CSB

When was the last time you really needed help? Whatever your needs are, God knows them, and he is there to help. The next time you feel like you don't know where to start, get on your knees and pray. Let God into every area of your life so you can figure it out together. When you get the help you need, you will be able to praise him and trust him even more.

God, I thank you today for all the help I have received from my friends and family in Christ. Thank you for placing people in my life who remind me of your love and grace, for without them I would be so much poorer.

Never Give Up

Love never gives up, never loses faith, is always hopeful,
and endures through every circumstance.

1 CORINTHIANS 13:7 NLT

You might not feel like you are the best witness of Christ's love even though you know this is one of our greatest commandments. Don't worry; you are not alone. It is hard to know where to begin in sharing your faith to others. Keep praying and developing your relationship with Jesus so you feel blessed, rather than ashamed, of your faith. Recognize that it is Jesus who helps you to never give up, to be hopeful, and to endure through every circumstance. Ask Jesus to help you come up with a way to express your faith.

Lord, may I rejoice in every trial. May I recognize that each one is for my refinement, and through them I can learn how to love even deeper. May my faith be forged in the fire and made stronger.

Eternal Food

"Why would you strive for food that is perishable and not be passionate to seek the food of eternal life, which never spoils? I, the Son of Man, am ready to give you what matters most, for God the Father has destined me for this purpose."

JOHN 6:27 TPT

When you go to Jesus in prayer, are you more like the crowd that demanded more food from him? Or are you a true disciple, coming to him for the bread that will satisfy? Though we don't want to admit it, it's easy to be like the crowd. We come before Jesus and ask for temporary things, for things that spoil. Ask for thankfulness and contentment in Him, truly believing that he is all you need to be satisfied.

Lord, you are satisfaction to the unsatisfied, and comfort to the afflicted. You fill me up when I am empty. I long for you every day, hoping for your grace and love to wash over me.

Laugh at Days Ahead

She laughs without fear of the future.
PROVERBS 31:25 NLT

Trouble will come to every life. It's not *if*; it's *when*. How can we prepare for the troubles that lie ahead? We certainly can't trouble-proof our lives, but we can build our faith by immersing ourselves in the Word of God, by spending time in prayer and trusting God's magnificent promises. There's an old saying: "Forewarned is forearmed." A wise person is prepared—armed with the Word of God and ready for whatever comes.

God, I long for your Word. I long for the time spent meditating on your Scriptures and their meaning. Prepare me for the future with your promises. Let them surround me like a hedge, and I will be safe.

No One Else

"No one is holy like the LORD!
There is no one besides you;
there is no Rock like our God."

1 SAMUEL 2:2 NLT

Let us never forget God's goodness in our lives and honor him whenever he comes through for us in faithfulness. There truly is no one holy like the Lord. He is our rock, our deliverer, our loyal defender, and our God. He answers the prayers of his people. Pour out your heart to him; he will surprise you with his goodness as you look to him.

Who is good but you, God? There is no other like you in holiness and glory. I will plant my feet upon you as my rock of salvation, for all other ground is shifting sand. You are my only refuge in times of tribulation.

Not Abandoned

I spoke hastily when I said, "The Lord has deserted me."
For in truth, you did hear my prayer and came to rescue me.

PSALM 31:22 TPT

It's not natural for most of us to ask for help. We try to push through and do things on our own, proudly wearing the badge of independence. Asking for help takes humility. Did you know that humility in the kingdom of God is like gold? It's a quality to be admired and sought after. We need to be humble enough to ask for help—from others and from God.

Lord, I know that every good horse acknowledges nudges from its master. May I be the same. When I feel as though I am alone, may I feel you nudging me to stay on the path. May I not lose heart nor be dismayed.

Bring Down Walls

The LORD is near to the brokenhearted
and saves the crushed in spirit.
PSALM 34:18 ESV

Feeling lonely or isolated can be one of the worst feelings in the world. Sometimes we are physically alone, which makes sense to us why we would feel lonely, but other times even in crowds the feeling can creep in. Some of us isolate to avoid pain, and others are removed because of grief or depression. None of these are walls too great to keep the Lord away. He can break down any barrier to get to his children. If the walls feel too high, simply cry out his name. That prayer has enough power to bring down the walls.

Lord, you are near to me when I am crushed by the weight of this world. May I not lose heart. May I hold on in the difficulty and not give up. Thank you for the promise that you reward those who continue in faith.

Never in Vain

Yahweh, you have heard the desires of the humble
and seen their hopes.
You will hear their cries and encourage their hearts.

PSALM 10:17 TPT

God wants us to communicate with him in prayer. When we cry out to him, it is never in vain. He is willing and able to answer our prayers. The problem is that we don't pray! Is our first thought when we need help to ask Jesus? That is a habit all Christians need to develop because he is near to those who cry out to him. Prayer develops our relationship with God, and it shows us more of his character. Try to make a habit of praying wherever you are.

Show your love, beloved Lord. Do not let your people feel as though they are alone. All around me I see discouragement and despair, yet I know that you are a God of hope and you can revitalize the dying.

Not to Us

Not to us, LORD,
not to us but to your name be the glory,
because of your love and faithfulness.

PSALM 115:1 NIV

It's easy to accept the accolades of people when things you have been involved in have gone well. We like our ideas and plans to succeed, and we like to be acknowledged for the good we have done. But things can start to become self-inflated when we give ourselves too much credit and become puffed up with pride. It's always more important to remember where your success came from—the goodness and grace of God in your life. You can accept praise but pass it on to the one who is truly worthy because we really can do nothing good without him.

God, I choose to glorify you this day. When offers of prestige and honor are given to me, I will pass it to you, for anything good I have done is from you. You are the great architect of every good accomplishment.

Numbers

"They will be as numerous as the sacred flocks that fill Jerusalem's streets at the time of her festivals. The ruined cities will be crowded with people once more, and everyone will know that I am the LORD."

EZEKIEL 36:38 NLT

Have you felt a sense of stirring in your day that God is about to do something new in your life? It is time for celebrating what the Lord is doing and what he promises to do with you. Spend some time preparing for the flourishing times ahead. Pray for passion, pray for others to join you, pray for lives that will be changed. Let God fill your heart with joy in the hope of a new season.

Be at work, Holy Spirit. I pray for revival; I pray for a new season. There is the desire for change in my heart, and I want to see something new happen. May your Spirit wash over this place, bringing new life and joy.

Oceans

You rule the raging of the sea;
when its waves rise, you still them.

PSALM 89:9 ESV

If you've ever had the privilege of booking a vacation near the ocean, you'll know the most expensive rooms are those with ocean views. We love to look at the vastness of the ocean, the deep blue of the waters, and watch the rise and fall of the waves. We might enjoy watching others surf, seeing the skill of how they move across the water. How different an experience it is when you are in that same water! The waves that crashed so beautifully on the shore are the same waves that dump you on the sand. The sea has a sense of raging, but this is nothing in comparison to the Creator of the waves. Trust in him today.

Lord, you have created both the valley and the mountain. You are the creator of both the calm and the storm. I know you rule the raging of the seas, so rule the raging of my heart. It is beyond my control but not beyond yours.

Unbroken Gratitude

What can I offer the LORD for all he has done for me?
I will lift up the cup of salvation
and praise the LORD's name for saving me.
I will keep my promises to the LORD
in the presence of all his people.

PSALM 116:12-14 NLT

When God saves us, what is our reaction? Are we overwhelmed with gratitude, or do we easily forget and move on without thought? We don't deserve his grace, yet he continues to give it. We've become so accustomed to him faithfully meeting our needs and coming to our aid, that we may take him for granted. We are spoiled in his love, and we still demand more. Our hearts are in desperate need of cultivation of humility so gratitude can pour out often and freely.

Nothing I have received from you is my due. Father, you have bestowed your grace upon me when I did not deserve it. I pray that your name would be exalted this day and you would be recognized as the author of salvation.

Only Pray

He shall pray to God, and He will delight in him,
He shall see His face with joy,
For He restores to man His righteousness.

JOB 33:26 NKJV

Can you imagine if everyone you encountered found you utterly delightful? For most of us, such a favored time in our lives ended around the age of two. Yet, no baby is preoccupied with how to make people like them. The only one worthy of such effort is the Lord, and, amazingly, he is the only one who doesn't place conditions on us becoming part of his friend group. He restores, welcomes, and loves. We need only to pray.

Bring restoration to these dry bones, Lord. I pray for your welcoming love to embrace my sojourning soul, for I have passed through desert after desert, and I long for home. I long for heaven, and for your embrace.

Open Door

Pray for us, too, that God may open a door for our message, so that we may proclaim the mystery of Christ, for which I am in chains. Pray that I may proclaim it clearly, as I should.

COLOSSIANS 4:3-4 NIV

We should always pray that God will open doors for us to share his message. You might not be in a distant land to proclaim the gospel, or in chains for trying to preach the good news, but there are plenty of people who are. Think of those people who are intent on furthering the kingdom and devote yourself to praying for them.

Lord, I pray for those who are in chains for your gospel. I pray that you would renew them, turning them from despair to hope. Please open a door for them to share your Word. May they know that the body of Christ has not forgotten them.

Opportunity to Praise

Let everything that breathes
praise the LORD.
Praise the LORD!

PSALM 150:6 NCV

With every breath we breathe, we have an opportunity to praise the Lord. It need not be with shouts or songs. It can be with quiet thanks and a heart of gratitude. It can be as simple as remembering you are seen and known by the Creator of all things. It can be as miniscule as a moment of acknowledgment of his presence with you. Whatever it is that nourishes and keeps you in this moment can be an avenue for gratitude if you let it be.

Lord, I thank you today for the air I breathe, the water I drink, and the life that fills my being. Thank you most of all for the sacrifice you made on the cross and for the love you have displayed toward me.

Father in Heaven

The Lord sees all we do;
he watches over his friends day and night.
His godly ones receive the answers they seek
whenever they cry out to him.

PSALM 34:15 TPT

Do we know in the depths of our hearts that our prayers are heard: both the shouting cries for help and the gentle whispers of thanksgiving? He knows our every thought before we even think it. This is the Father who created us and calls us by name. We are his beloved children. We need to let the truth sink into the very deepest parts of our hearts and rest there in thanksgiving. His Word is truth, and he tells us time and time again that he will answer our prayer because we trust in him.

God, what a glory it is to be your friend. I stand amazed that you, perfect in glory and perfection, want to know me and pursue me. May your name forever be praised and your renown reach the ends of the earth.

Our Present Hope

Through Christ you have come to trust in God. And you have placed your faith and hope in God because he raised Christ from the dead and gave him great glory.

1 PETER 1:21 NLT

God raised Christ Jesus from the dead and seated him at his right hand. From this place, Jesus makes intercession for us. He has also raised us up to sit with him in heavenly places! Assured of this hope, we can daily sit with Jesus and agree with him in prayer. We can be confident that Jesus will perfect all that concerns us as we pray in unity with him for his purposes to be established. He can and will do above and beyond what we ask or imagine, according to the power that works in us.

Just as you raised your Son, please raise me up from death to life, heavenly Father. Take my corrupt, broken soul and let it die, so it may be buried and resurrected with Jesus Christ.

Overconfident

"Watch and pray so that you will not fall into temptation.
The spirit is willing, but the body is weak."

MATTHEW 26:41 NIV

"You had one job!" It's an exclamation said as a joke, but it's often used to point out that someone had a simple thing to do and failed to do it. In the garden of Gethsemane, the disciples had one job from Jesus: to stay awake and pray. Jesus knew what was coming. He knew that the greatest crisis he would ever face was on its way. He understood that soon he would be crucified. The disciples, however, didn't see it coming. When things are going well, we can get too confident and rely on our own strength. Don't stop praying! In good times and bad, let Jesus be your confidence.

Lord, whether I am sure or doubtful, you are my confidence. You are the friend at my side and the shield in front of me. When the enemy attacks, I know that I have you to rely on. May I not grow weak in prayer.

Party Time

"Suppose a woman has ten silver coins and loses one…when she finds it, she will call in her friends and neighbors and say, 'Rejoice with me because I have found my lost coin.' In the same way, there is joy in the presence of God's angels when even one sinner repents."

LUKE 15:8-10 NLT

If you could throw a party for your closest friends, what kind of party would you have? What kind of party you choose says a lot about what you like. God has a party preference too. He loves welcome-to-my-family parties. Every time someone turns away from their sin and asks God for new life, God and the angels celebrate. Share the good news of Jesus with those around you. It just might result in giving God a great reason to celebrate!

God, I pray for new family members. I pray that my spiritual family would grow both as I come to know more of your children and as you bring more people into your family. I long for them to know you.

Patient Decision

"Be strong and courageous! Do not be afraid and do not panic before them. For the LORD your God will personally go ahead of you. He will neither fail you nor abandon you."

DEUTERONOMY 31:6

Emergency situations demand emergency responses. EMTs are skilled in remaining calm when decisions need to be made in seconds. Sometimes we think we need to do the same with life decisions. Should we take the job, move, grasp whatever opportunity lies before us, or run to find another open door? When we make decisions out of panic and rush, we often trust our own wisdom and judgment. What if we paused and prayed instead? What if we gave it five minutes, a day, or a week. To release control is no easy task, but letting God lead is always best.

Lord, I give you control. Take my life, take my difficulties, take my hardships, and make them into something beautiful for your glory. Make me your humble servant, willing to follow you through trials.

Waiting

I wait for the LORD, my soul waits,
and in his word I hope.

PSALM 130:5 ESV

We live in a fast culture: instant messaging, fast-food, high-speed internet, and automated everything! The quicker, the better. Waiting is not on our list of favorite things to do. We are used to getting things done in an efficient fashion, yet when we pray, God seems to be on an entirely different timetable. He often asks us to wait. Why? Because God is more interested in developing our character than he is in instant messaging. Patience, endurance, faithfulness, and perseverance are developed in the waiting.

Lord, I pray for your action. Not by my own strength, but by yours. I have no one to rely on but you. I will not give up or cease to pray, for I have seen how those who knock on your door are not dismayed.

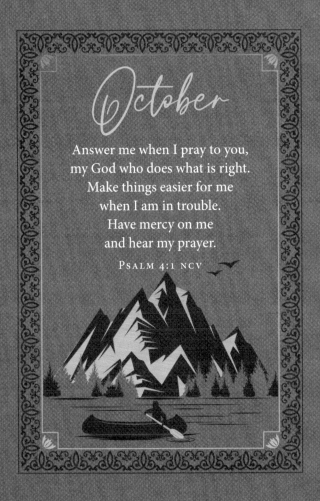

October

Answer me when I pray to you,
my God who does what is right.
Make things easier for me
when I am in trouble.
Have mercy on me
and hear my prayer.

PSALM 4:1 NCV

Pause

As I thought of you I moaned,
"God, where are you?"
I'm overwhelmed with despair
as I wait for your help to arrive.
Pause in his presence.

PSALM 77:3 TPT

There are times in life where there is no silver lining. We cannot create goodness out of what looks like desolation and destruction. It is not a failure to be desperate. When we can't see how anything can grow out of the devastation of our lives, we do not need to pretend to be hopeful. Let us come to God, asking him the questions that lurk in the corners of our mind. This is an invitation to remember who God is. Not who he was or will be, but who he is right now. Let's take a cue from the Psalmist and pause in God's presence.

Where are you when I feel alone, God? Why have I known the evils I have known? Please, God Almighty, reach down from heaven and touch my heart. Give me the faith to continue when there is no answer.

Paying the Bills

"There is no need to imitate them, since your Father already
knows what you need before you ask him."

MATTHEW 6:8 TPT

Not only can making ends meet keep us awake at night,
but the worry can also make us miserable. How will we
pay the bills? What if we can't make the house payment?
How will we live? Financial stress can cause anxiety. God
knows our needs even before we ask. He does not always
supply in miraculous ways, but he is never surprised by
our needs. He is our provider, and he wants us to bring our
financial worries to him. We can rest knowing he is aware of
everything we need even before we ask.

*Lord, as long as I am still alive, I pray that I would be at
peace with what I have. I do not always feel as though I have
enough, but I know that you do not forget those who take
refuge in you. You always provide.*

Perfect Timing

A time to tear and a time to mend,
a time to be silent and a time to speak.

ECCLESIASTES 3:7 NIV

Everything in its time. We've heard it, and we've likely said it, but how willingly do we embrace it? If there's a snag in a relationship, are we secure in our understanding of whether it should be unraveled or stitched back together? Even when we know what to do, don't we sometimes allow pride, history, or other people's opinions influence our decision? What a comfort it is to take these questions to our Lord. The answer he gives will always be right. His timing can always be trusted.

Lord of wisdom, you have no lack of understanding. You know my situation, and you know what future lies ahead of me. Give me a path to walk on. May it be one that honors you and recognizes your sovereignty.

Persist

Our hope for you is firmly grounded,
knowing that as you are partners in our sufferings,
so also you are in our comfort.

2 CORINTHIANS 1:7 NASB

We can get weary of praying the same request for years.
Waiting for someone we are discipling to really commit
to giving Jesus control of their lives can be discouraging.
Some days we just want to throw in the towel. If we believe
Scripture, we will soldier on. God promises that if we persist,
we'll see the evidence of our faith. It might be hard and
exhausting, but if we're doing it to serve Christ, it will be
worth the work.

*Jesus, teach me to wake up with my mind turned toward
you, and to do the work of your mission. I know that it has a
reward beyond wealth and comfort, so help me not to neglect
its completion.*

Petitions

"Hear the prayers and petitions of your servant. For your sake, Lord, look with favor on your desolate sanctuary. Give ear, our God, and hear; open your eyes and see the desolation of the city that bears your Name. We do not make requests of you because we are righteous, but because of your great mercy."

DANIEL 9:17-18 NIV

Are you waiting for a breakthrough in your circumstances? Maybe you have been praying for an unbelieving family member, a strained relationship, an answer to your financial stress, or clarity for a big decision ahead. Fasting doesn't often top the list of what to do when you really need that breakthrough, and it's not that hard to guess why it isn't a popular option. Consider what the Bible says about fasting and notice how it goes hand in hand with prayer. Fasting requires sobriety of heart, reflection, and focus. It tells the Lord that you are ready to receive his revelation and guidance.

Lord, it is not for my sake alone that your plan exists. I see that it is ultimately for your glory and for your recognition. May the whole earth bend the knee and praise your name.

The Antidote

"Don't let your hearts be troubled.
Trust in God, and trust also in me."

JOHN 14:1 NLT

The human heart has a propensity toward worry. What will happen if or when? Anxiety is like a seed of fear that, when nurtured, fed, and watered, develops into an organism that devours the life-giving promises in God's Word. It is so comforting to know that God provides an antidote, a pesticide of sorts, which will eradicate the paralyzing seedlings of anxiety—trust in him. He will gladly help us when we ask.

Still, Lord, make me still. Give me peace, slow my heart, and make me see that you are always in control. I am troubled greatly in my soul, so make your mercy appear greater to me than it ever has before.

Please Answer

Turn and answer me, O Lord my God!
Restore the sparkle to my eyes, or I will die.

PSALM 13:3 NLT

There's an age old saying that the eyes are the window to the soul. You can probably describe those times when you looked in someone's eyes and saw sadness, pain, or regret. Equally, eyes show joy and contentment—what we might refer to as a sparkle. Going through tough times can take that sparkle away. When you lose hope, joy, or peace, your eyes will tell the story. You may feel that in this moment your joy has slipped away from you. Ask the Lord to turn and answer you. Ask him for hope. Ask him to restore that spark of life so you might live life fully.

Sometimes it seems as though every day is spent in hurt and agony. I lose the desire for life, and no comfort appeals to me. If you have hope in reserve for me, please give it to me now, Lord. I am at my end, and only you can restore me.

Position for Rescue

I am dying from grief;
my years are shortened by sadness.
Sin has drained my strength;
I am wasting away from within.
PSALM 31:10 NLT

Imagine yourself in a hurricane. It's too late to evacuate on your own and the floodwaters are rising. Do you sit in your house on the floor level, watching TV and hoping someone will find you? No! You go up on the roof and wait for help. It's the same in our spiritual lives. When life's storms come, it's not helpful to continue on with business as usual, trying to convince ourselves, God, and others that we are fine. When the storms come, we need to position ourselves for rescue. We need to move into a posture of prayer and worship. God is faithful to rescue us.

Lord, send your redemption. Rescue me from the pit of death I feel trapped in. Is there anyone besides you who can rescue me? Whether it be through a friend or some other way, please send your redemption.

Powerful Kingdom

The kingdom of God is not in words,
but in power.

1 CORINTHIANS 4:20 NASB

How have you seen the power of God at work in your life? Have you ever witnessed a miracle that could not be explained away? God's power works in both the tiny details of our lives and in great and mysterious ways. The kingdom of God is not found in our theories or ideologies about faith. It is as real as the ground beneath our feet. Do you have any longings or needs that require a move of God? Pour out your heart before him today and invite him to move in power.

Lord, what are my words, that they should do anything? Surely they are just wind without you moving within me. Please be at work within me and around me, making your justice shine like the noonday.

Gratitude Focus

Praise the LORD!
I will thank the LORD with all my heart
as I meet with his godly people.

PSALM 111:1 NLT

There is power in gratitude not because it has some magical force, but because it directs our focus toward the blessings that are already ours. It is good not only to make a private practice of gratitude, but also to be intentional about it with others. The next time you are with a friend, a coworker, or a family member, make a point to share something that you are grateful for—including them! Encouragement is a gift to everyone. Let this be the day you lean into the vulnerability of sharing what you love about people with them.

Jesus, I pray today that you would teach me to show my gratitude around others in an uplifting way. May they know that I love them and appreciate them, and may I not be reluctant in such gratitude.

Let Hope Arise

Let all that I am praise the LORD.
I will praise the LORD as long as I live.
I will sing praises to my God with my dying breath.

PSALM 146:1-2 NLT

God commands us numerous times in his Word to praise him. But on some days, digging through the rubble to find a nugget of gratitude seems flat out formidable. Negative thoughts float through the mind like a shadowy cloud, and if allowed to remain, can darken the entire day. The Psalmist understood. Even though his life was in constant danger, he knew that as he centered on the greatness of God, his problems would be divinely solved. Make David's words your own prayer to the Lord this morning. As you do, hope will arise.

Lord, I pray that every part of my being would praise you. I pray that as long as there is breath in my lungs I would sing your praises, shouting your fame until the day my soul departs from this earth.

What Wins

Through the praise of children and infants
you have established a stronghold against your enemies,
to silence the foe and the avenger.

PSALM 8:2 NIV

Whenever God chooses to use the weak things of this world rather than the strong, he proves that true strength comes only from him. When Christ came as a baby into this world, he terrified the powers of earth through Herod as well as the armies of Hades! They knew their days of reigning and oppressing were numbered. Praising God goes a long way toward actual change in the conditions of our hearts. Sometimes we overcomplicate things or try to control more than we should. Our dependence on God and appreciation of him is pleasing to him.

God, am I strong in my own eyes? Am I wise in my own eyes? If so, please change me. Be my boast, be my strength. Be my everything, for I know that without you, all things are weak and foolish.

Praising Together

You are enthroned as the Holy One;
you are the one Israel praises.

PSALM 22:3 NIV

When was the last time you were a part of a church service?
For some it is every week; for others it is more sporadic.
This habitual attendance might seem a little religious, and
yet there is something to be said about coming together
and worshipping God as a group of people. He deserves the
corporate praise of his people.

You are my King, yet you are also the King of so many others.
I pray that I would not be isolated in my worship. Please give
me a community of believers to shout your praises with.

Crossing Warden

Arise, LORD!
Lift up your hand, O God.
Do not forget the helpless.

PSALM 10:12 NIV

When you are driving around a school zone, you might see crossing wardens who put up their hand to stop you from driving while children are crossing. There is so much trouble and injustice in this world that sometimes we just want God to raise his hand and put a stop to it all. Why doesn't our good God prevent things from happening? Instead of questioning God's goodness, we can pray the prayer of the Psalmist—that we would see an end to all the wrong in this life.

Lord, where is the justice? My eyes grow tired from weeping, for the corruption and brokenness in this world weighs down my conscience. Please, God, do not forget the helpless. Stand up for the orphan and defend the widow.

Pray Boldly

"If you can?" said Jesus.
"Everything is possible for one who believes."
MARK 9:23 NIV

When you pray, are you doing it in a spirit of boldness, or are you praying weak prayers? It's as if we are afraid to bother God with our requests. We better not pester him too much, or perhaps he won't answer, right? Let's stop with the weak prayers. You're not a wimp; you're a child of God! The Lord knows your heart already. Believe that he can do what you are asking. There is no need for caution with the Father who loves you so dearly. Jesus said so himself.

Lord, I fear that sometimes I do not truly believe what I read in your Word. I believe you, but not as much as I should. Please take my unbelief and vanquish it by the testimony of what you have done.

For All People

First, I tell you to pray for all people. Ask God for the things people need, and be thankful to him. You should pray for kings and for all who have authority. Pray for the leaders so that we can have quiet and peaceful lives—lives full of worship and respect for God.

1 TIMOTHY 2:1-2 NLT

Prayer is a powerful connection between us and God. It releases the power of his kingdom into our lives. It connects our hearts to the unending and all-consuming love of Jesus. There is nothing too insignificant to pray about. There is nothing too complex for him either, so let's not hold back from asking God to bring breakthrough in impossible situations. Sometimes, it is in the struggle of praying for those we do not like or respect that transformation takes place in our hearts.

God, help me to persevere in prayer. I pray over those in my life who do not know you, that you would make yourself known to them. Please also encourage all my brothers and sisters in Christ who suffer for your name. Please sustain them.

Lifting Up Leaders

This is good and pleases God our Savior, who wants everyone to be saved and to understand the truth.

1 TIMOTHY 2:3 NLT

Good results come from having good people in leadership. As you have prayed and perhaps even encouraged a leader, remember that it isn't just for the benefit of the leader, but it is also for the benefit of a community. God finds all kinds of ways to show himself to others, and one of these ways will be through Christlike leaders. Be confident that your support encourages the gospel to spread.

Lord, today I lift up the leaders both in the faith and outside of it. I pray over the politicians leading our country, over the pastors leading your Church, and over everyone else with an administrative role. Please anoint them with humility and strength.

Remembered in Prayer

> I have not stopped giving thanks to God for you.
> I always remember you in my prayers.
>
> EPHESIANS 1:16 NCV

Paul prayed for the body of Christ so we would succeed, collectively and individually. As we know God better, we are enlightened in the hope of our inheritance. We press on in faith, knowing that God has already empowered us and crushed the enemy under our feet. We are able and free to glorify God. We pray for others so they will see his goodness and praise him as well.

Father God, please bless those who display your testimony to this world. Without them, I do not know what I would do. I pray that these friends, who have blessed others so many times, would in turn be blessed by you.

Hope in Power

Surely no one lays a hand on a broken man
when he cries for help in his distress.
Have I not wept for those in trouble?
Has not my soul grieved for the poor?

JOB 30:24-25 NIV

When our hearts hurt for those who are suffering, or when
we are sensitive to things that are not right, our hearts are
close to God's. There are a lot of hard things in this life. It
is important to remember that Jesus cares about our pain.
Broken homes, lack of food, abuse, and sickness are just a
few of the problems that our world faces. Instead of getting
sad about a hopeless situation, we can find hope in the
power of Jesus. Pray with hope, act with hope, and spread
hope to the world around you.

*God, I pray that you would make me a beacon of hope for
those who are in distress. May the crippled, the broken,
and the depressed find in me a friend and a bearer of your
wonderful testimony.*

Rescue Plea

O Lord my God, I cried to you for help,
and you have healed me.

Psalm 30:2 esv

The ancient people used the word *healing* to mean more than just an answer to a physical problem. Pain extends beyond our body's bruises, illness, and disease. We experience pain on an emotional, mental, and sometimes even spiritual level. All of these discomforts cause us to cry out for help; it is mostly in our distress that we are led toward a plea to be rescued. What kind of pain are you facing today? Have confidence in this Scripture that assures us that we will be healed.

Lord, when I was in distress, you were there. When I walked through the darkest valley, you were there. You have been with me all the way, lifting me up when I fall and guiding me along the path toward heaven.

Power of Prayer

God knows how often I pray for you. Day and night I bring
you and your needs in prayer to God, whom I serve with all
my heart by spreading the Good News about his Son.

ROMANS 1:9 NLT

Prayer is powerful. You might have heard that from a
preacher, or from a friend who is passionate about prayer.
But you might not feel like prayer is powerful. You might
have been disappointed by times when you have prayed and
seemingly nothing has happened. A lack of results doesn't
negate the power of prayer. Prayer brings you closer to
Jesus because you begin to converse with him. It opens your
heart and shows that you need him. It helps you think about
others instead of being so focused on yourself. Restore your
confidence today by praying for others and feel the power of
prayer changing you.

*Lord, I pray that you would be at work in the lives of those
I see around me, not just those who are close to me, but also
the strangers I meet on the street and the people I only see
for a few seconds at a time. Please change the course of their
lives to be in line with your heart.*

I Do Believe

Immediately the boy's father exclaimed,
"I do believe; help me overcome my unbelief!"

MARK 9:24 NIV

Do you believe that God can make things possible in your life? We know that he's not a genie, granting every wish, but he is a good Father who wants the best for you. Step out boldly in faith, beginning with your prayer life. Are you talking to God in a spirit of timidity? Ask him for help in overcoming your disbelief. Everything is possible for those who believe, so set your heart upon doing so.

God, why do I question your power? Why do I have these doubts that creep into my heart? I pray today that you would cast them out and show me the way, changing me from a mindset of timidity to one of boldness.

Proclaim His Name

"I will proclaim the name of the LORD;
ascribe greatness to our God!"

DEUTERONOMY 32:3 ESV

The start of a new day can mark a time for new beginnings in your heart. As you prepare for the day ahead, remember the greatness of your God. Take some time to read your favorite Scripture or listen to worship music. When you allow yourself to dwell on the wonder of God, your lips can't help but proclaim his name.

How great you are, my Savior and Redeemer. You have parted the sea and made a way for me. You have leveled the mountain and raised the valley so I may pass through. As long as I live, may my lips praise your name!

Promised Grace

I entreated Your favor with my whole heart;
Be merciful to me according to Your word.

PSALM 119:58 NKJV

Do you feel God's nearness on a daily basis? As you reflect on this, ask yourself if there were recent moments of experiencing God's mercy or blessing? Take time to direct your whole heart toward him. Tell God all about your week: the small things, the annoying things, the humorous things. It is all part of who you are, and as you share your whole heart, you just might see where God has shown his favor to you.

Have my whole heart, Lord. Take the oddities, the strengths, the weaknesses, and the boring parts. I pray that you would take it and transform it, molding it into your image. Dwell richly within me.

Adoration

How right they are to adore you.

SONG OF SOLOMON 1:4 NLT

People worship Jesus when they sing, dance, and exclaim the adoration they have for him. Some may wonder why, but Jesus is definitely worthy of our praise and adoration. He is perfect, loving, kind, gentle, just—and that's only a few of his attributes. It is right that the church throughout generations praises him. He is the one who saves. Take time today to adore him for who he is.

How good it is to see a congregation praising your name, Jesus. You are perfect and holy, abounding in love and righteousness. I see now that it is only right for every creature to lift up and praise your name.

Purposeful Life

In their hearts humans plan their course,
but the LORD establishes their steps.

PROVERBS 16:9 NIV

As you pray today, listen closely to what God might want you to add or cut out of your schedule. Listen for relationships that need tending and forgiveness that needs to be given. God is in the day-to-day just as much as he is in the big moments. Find a characteristic of God you want to learn more about. Do you want to see his mercy splashed over your week? Do you want to notice his goodness working all around you? Make an attribute of God a priority for you today, and you'll sense his blessing all over your plans.

Father God, please establish my steps. Take all the little details of my life and sanctify them for your purpose. There is so much that I cannot keep a handle on, and so much out of my control. Please, be sovereign over it all.

Quietly Waiting

For God alone, O my soul,
wait in silence,
for my hope is from him.

PSALM 62:5 ESV

If the radio were broken in your car, would you need to fix
it immediately, or would you relish the silence? Perhaps
you or someone you know keeps the TV on all day "for the
noise." What is it about silence that makes so many of us
uncomfortable? Some of us even talk to ourselves to avoid it.
Seek out silence today. Allow God to discern your needs and
your questions, and then wait for him to answer.

*Lord God, today I lay out for you my questions, my doubts,
my hidden pain, and all that is within me. Take it all and
discern my thoughts and motives. Reveal them to me and
show me your plan.*

Radiance

Those who look to him are radiant with joy;
their faces will never be ashamed.

PSALM 34:5 CSB

Life is full of decisions—big and small. Your personality
might be one that likes to make swift decisions, or you
may be someone who deliberates carefully over the right
choice. Our brains are all wired differently. God designed
you uniquely, yet he never intended that you would have to
make decisions on your own. Are you facing some important
decisions right now? Look to God to help you in the process;
he knows what will make you shine!

*Lord, help me keep my eyes on you. When distractions arise
and life gets busy, please keep my eyes on you. Not to the
right nor to the left, Lord, but to you. Keep my heart focused
on your radiance, and I shall not be ashamed.*

Reflections

As in water face reflects face,
so the heart of man reflects the man.
PROVERBS 27:19 ESV

Waking up in the morning, one of the first things you may do is rub your eyes, put on your slippers, and walk down the hall to the bathroom. In the bathroom, most of us have a mirror so we can watch as we wash our faces. In the same way we use the mirror to check our appearance, our soul is visible through the state of our heart. God has given us the mirrors of prayer and the Bible to expose our hearts. We can ignore what we see and walk away, or we can respond. We might not be able to change our outward reflection, but God gives us the opportunity to change the one inside.

Who am I, really? Sometimes I do not know, God. Please show me a reflection of who I am, and who you want me to be. Show me all the ways I have left to grow. Only through you will I reach perfection.

Join in Song

Shout for joy, you heavens!
Earth, rejoice!
Mountains break forth into joyful shots!
For the Lord has comforted his people,
and will have compassion on his afflicted ones.

ISAIAH 49:13 CSB

Our greatest certainty in life is the presence of the Living God. Still, you may join with many who have asked how suffering and God's goodness can co-exist. Though we all must wrestle through the facts of suffering in the world, we have a God who suffered with us and for us. Let's not get stuck on repeat. Let our song ring out about the comfort that the Lord gives, about the compassion that he wraps around us. The song of suffering might seem loud, but the earth declares even louder the comfort and compassion of our risen Savior. Join in the singing!

Oh Lord, if only I could hear the great cacophony of your whole creation giving praise! If only every bird, every mountain, river, and cloud would sing your praises with me as they were made to. May your name be exalted today.

Remain Upright

A righteous person falls seven times and rises again,
But the wicked stumble in time of disaster.

PROVERBS 24:16 NASB

God gives us our tenacity. When we meet someone who has
none, the most loving thing we can do for them is pray, and
make sure we tell them about the source of our strength—
the source of all hope. A heart that doesn't know God is
too easily broken. A soul without his strength is too easily
crushed. Praying for words that reach their wounded spirits,
let us make sure we never leave someone on the ground
without them knowing who picked us up.

*Lord, I pray that I would learn to always give you the credit
you deserve for my salvation. May those around me know
who has saved me and who is responsible for the comfort I
have. Blessed be your name.*

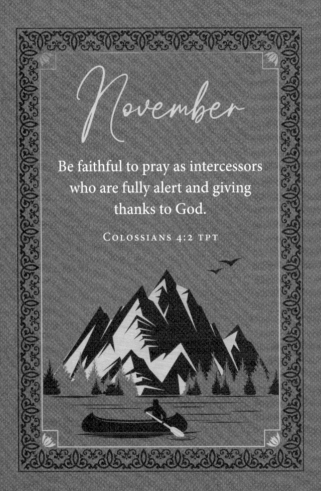

November

Be faithful to pray as intercessors
who are fully alert and giving
thanks to God.

COLOSSIANS 4:2 TPT

Reputation

I will remember the deeds of the LORD;
yes, I will remember your miracles of long ago.
I will consider all your works and meditate
on all your mighty deeds.

PSALM 77:11-12 NIV

The reputation of a person is based on the beliefs and opinions people hold about that person. Even God has a reputation. People base what they think about him on their past experiences, their interactions with believers, and what they have seen in and around church. The tricky part is that a reputation isn't always accurate. It's based on perception. That's why it's important that we, as believers, remember all the miracles God has done. When we remember the great deeds of God and share them with others, it helps people, including ourselves, create an accurate picture of who God is.

Lord, your great deeds precede you. The earth stands as an example of your faithful love toward every generation. You bless me in more ways than I will ever understand, so I praise you with every breath I take.

Respect and Fear

Let us be thankful, because we have a kingdom that cannot be shaken. We should worship God in a way that pleases him with respect and fear.

HEBREWS 12:28 NCV

How much of our prayers are worship and adoration of our Holy God? He has already given us more than we can comprehend. Bringing our requests and fears to the Lord is not wrong; in fact, he urges us to. But if the only time we go to the Lord is in supplication, then our relationship with him is only as deep as our perceived need. The Mighty One, the Maker of heaven and earth, love and life, is worthy of our praise and thanksgiving. When we give to God purely out of the gratitude of our hearts, he finds a way to give right back to us.

God, thank you for the unshakeable kingdom which you have founded for eternity. There is no other like you in might and glory. In light of your greatness, I will praise you with a full heart.

Reverence

Those who feared the LORD talked with each other, and the LORD listened and heard. A scroll of remembrance was written in his presence concerning those who feared the LORD and honored his name.

MALACHI 3:16 NIV

Many people disregard the kindness of God, ignoring his gift of salvation. They use his name, but only as a swear word. This breaks his heart. When his children show reverence for him and offer prayers of thanksgiving and songs of praise, he is immensely pleased. God remembers those who acknowledge him for the loving, just God that he is. When we receive Christ, he writes our name in the book of life, a guarantee that we belong to him and will be accepted into his kingdom because of the sacrifice of Jesus. We are his, and he is ours.

You are my God, and I am your son. You have brought me out of a life of sin and into a life of redemption, surrounding me with a family of believers and fellow worshipers. I pray that I would honor your name with every moment.

Rhetorical or Not

"LORD, the God of our ancestors,
are you not the God who is in heaven?
You rule over all the kingdoms of the nations.
Power and might are in your hand,
and no one can withstand you."

2 CHRONICLES 20:6 NIV

There are times for rhetorical questions, and times for real questions. We don't know what the writer of the Scripture was expressing, but it might be freeing to know that you can express doubts and certainty to God, and that all forms of your expression can actually grow your faith. Perhaps you are in the middle of some personal turmoil right now. It's okay for you to ask if God is really sovereign. On the other hand, you may be experiencing a particular blessing that allows you to state, "Yes, God you are powerful and in control!" Whatever the situation, know that God can withstand your doubts and will delight in your praise.

Lord, you are powerful, so I know I can trust you with my honest doubts. At times, I am faced with a mountain of disbelief, and I am more cynical than hopeful. Please meet me in this place, and answer my doubts.

Always Near

By awesome deeds you answer us with righteousness,
O God of our salvation,
the hope of all the ends of the earth
and of the farthest seas.

PSALM 65:5 ESV

What have you been asking of God lately? It could be healing
from illness, prayer for someone close to you who is hurting,
or maybe you just need a little help in your relationships.
God can sometimes seem very far away and unconcerned
with your requests and needs. These feelings, however, are
not the truth. The truth is that God is always very near to
you. He knows your heart, he knows what you need, and
he will answer. Trust him as you read this Scripture again
and know that he will answer your prayers with amazing
wonders and inspiring displays of power.

*Lord, I will place my faith in you. Coping mechanisms and
temptations surround me, but I will choose to look to you for
answers and comfort. You are my refuge in every storm and
difficulty.*

Righteous Prayers

Confess your sins to each other and pray for each other so that you may be healed. The earnest prayer of a righteous person has great power and produces wonderful results.

JAMES 5:16 NLT

It is never easy to confess our sins. When we have people around us who will stand by us in tough times, it is a lot easier. We should admit our sins to our brothers and sisters, so they can pray for us and help us through. By praying, checking in, and helping to find answers or alternatives, it becomes evident yet again that the body works best together with all its members. We were made to need each other. A righteous person who prays sincerely will surely see incredible results from the Lord. We want to be these people, and we want to know these people.

Purify me in righteousness, Jesus. Take my sinful, broken soul and make it new. I know that I am far from perfect, but I pray that you would bring me nearer to the image of who I was meant to be.

Good Answers

When one of your godly ones corrects me
or one of your faithful ones rebukes me,
I will accept it like an honor I cannot refuse.
It will be as healing medicine
that I swallow without an offended heart.
Even if they are mistaken,
I will continue to pray.

PSALM 141:5 TPT

You might not be the kind of person who takes advice easily. Perhaps you don't ask many people for help out of fear that they will say the wrong thing or maybe even offend you somehow. Be wise about who you share your heart with or ask input from. If they are full of the love of Christ, then their words should be honoring to him, and you will know deep down that what they are saying is right. Keep praying when you are in the middle of making decisions even if you feel like you have been given good answers. God is always guiding you, not just for the first step but every step of the way.

Lord, may I learn to excel in humility, so I do not refuse the rich rebukes which come from my brothers and sisters in Christ. They are not designed to bring me down, but rather, through your spirit of conviction, they can build me up.

Sacrifice of Praise

Let us offer through Jesus a continual sacrifice of praise to God, proclaiming our allegiance to his name. And don't forget to do good and to share with those in need. These are the sacrifices that please God.

HEBREWS 13:15-16 NLT

After being encouraged to hope for heaven rather than becoming overly anxious about worldly things, the persecuted Jews were told to offer a continual sacrifice of praise to God. Two ways of praising God and thanking him for restoring our lives are remaining faithful to him and helping those in need. Pompous and self-proclaiming religious acts do not impress God, but those who are faithful and extend love and service to others are greatly pleasing to him.

You are perfect in eternity, Lord. There is no one like you in glory and majesty. It is my honor to be called your son and to be called by your voice. May this not be a calling I keep to myself but one which I share.

Safety Guaranteed

He will keep you from every form of evil or calamity
as he continually watches over you.
You will be guarded by God himself.

PSALM 121:7 TPT

Even with modern engineering advancements, sheltering from a fierce storm can be troubling. There is no guarantee of safety. Would we sing for joy as we hunkered down? Rejoice in our place of refuge? If we were aware of the one who has promised to always protect, then our praises could indeed echo off the shelter walls! In the shadow of God's protection, we can be glad. He is the only one able to guarantee our safety!

What shepherd is there like you, perfect in protection and provision? Though other masters fail and have ulterior motives, you have proven yourself perfect in virtue and ability, Lord of Hosts!

Saving Grace

My soul, why would you be depressed?
Why would you sink into despair?
Just keep hoping and waiting on God, your Savior.
For no matter what, I will still sing with praise,
for you are my saving grace!

PSALM 42:5 TPT

When we're feeling low, it is hard to be motivated. We may find ourselves sinking into despair as we consider our circumstances. It is not failure to have a bad day or to feel overwhelmed; we don't need to feel shame about this. At the same time, we have been given the gift of leadership over our minds and hearts. When the troubles we face outweigh the hope we have, let us direct our gaze to the one who set the world in motion. He is still faithful. He is still working. He is still worthy. Today is an opportunity to praise him in the "not yet."

Lord, my goals lie ahead of me, not behind me. They have not found their completion yet, and I do not know if they will. But you are sovereign over failures and victories, and I will give both to you.

Secret Places

The secret of the LORD is for those who fear Him,
And He will make them know His covenant.

PSALM 25:14 NASB

Cherish the secret things. So much of our life is for others. Whether it is the requirement of jobs, keeping up relationships, or the programs we volunteer for, so much of our time and energy is spent on other people. God wants your time. He wants it for you and for him. Maybe this will require a designated prayer closet or a quiet place away. Cherish alone time with him today.

God, convict me of my priorities and idols. Is there something keeping me from you? Is there something I prioritize more than you? Where such things exist, make them clear to me, so I don't continue in sin.

Set Your Mind

To set the mind on the flesh is death,
but to set the mind on the Spirit is life and peace.

ROMANS 8:6 ESV

How can we set our minds on the Spirit? If you pray for help to be kinder to your co-worker, and then find yourself struggling with how to treat them later that day, pray again! Set your mind on the things of the Spirit moment by moment. You don't have to be in your prayer closet to communicate with the Spirit. He will help you and meet you throughout your day, giving you peace. Having open communication with God at all times will transform your mind and set it on him.

God, it is so easy to fall into a bad place in my mind. The world may be bright, but my mind is darkened at times by sin and corruption. Pull me up from this and do not let me be prey to the devil's schemes.

Shield of Faith

In all circumstances take up the shield of faith, with which you can extinguish all the flaming darts of the evil one.
EPHESIANS 6:16 ESV

Just as a shield was a key accessory to a soldier in ancient Rome, so our faith is to us today. We never know when the enemy will try to attack, so we must remain vigilant. The shield of faith is a big component to fighting and winning against the devil's onslaught. Without our faith, we are vulnerable, weak, and flawed humans. We're easy prey. It is God who makes us strong, for he alone can overcome the enemy. We must take up our shields and stand ready to use them by remaining in the Word, in prayer, and by staying attentive to what our Lord is saying.

Lord, guard me from the advances of the evil one. Place your shield in my arm so it stands between me and the temptations which assail me. No enemy can face your great strength, Lord of Hosts.

Shift of Focus

Don't worry, because I am with you.
Don't be afraid, because I am your God.
I will make you strong and will help you;
I will support you with my right hand that saves you.

ISAIAH 41:10 NCV

The subject of these verses is not us, it's God. When he is our source, we cannot fail. It's important to learn that we must shift our focus off ourselves and on to him. We could easily read this verse and make it all about us: how God will make us strong, help us, and lead us away from fear or worry. All of this is true and wonderful. But the real subject of these verses is God. He is doing all the work. God is our everything.

Your plan will be completed, and no one can stop it. Your strength knows no end, and your mercy is infinite in depth. Sweet Jesus, I praise you for folding me into your plan and sealing my future with your own.

Shout for Joy

May we shout for joy when we hear of your victory
and raise a victory banner in the name of our God.
May the LORD answer all your prayers.

PSALM 20:5 NLT

We often pray without expecting much of a response, so it
is good to acknowledge those times when we see that God
has answered our prayers. These Scriptures help to build our
faith and so do the stories of our answered prayers. They
are there to be shared. Be encouraged today to continue to
present your requests to God, knowing that he is listening.

*God, please fill my heart with joy on this day. I pray that the
shadows of this age would not dampen the fire which you
have placed within me. Let your light shine through me as a
lantern placed on a post for all to see.*

Showdown

Summon your power, God;
show us your strength, our God,
as you have done before.

PSALM 68:28 NIV

Four hundred prophets of Baal covered the mountain and began to dance and shout and even cut themselves. From morning until afternoon, they went on and on, begging their god to answer them. But nothing happened. No one answered. A single prophet of God stepped up to the top of the mountain. Elijah didn't dance or shout or cut himself. He did one thing—he prayed. Fire swooped down from the heaven and licked up the stones, the sacrifice, and all the water surrounding it. God had answered! The God that Elijah served and prayed to is the same God you pray to today. He is mighty to save!

God of Abraham, you have seen every age come and go. Your infinite gaze stretches from the beginning of this earth's existence until its end. I trust you, for you have remained the same from age to age.

Thank You

I, with shouts of grateful praise, will sacrifice to you.
What I have vowed I will make good.
I will say, "Salvation comes from the LORD."

JONAH 2:9 NIV

When you're young, your parents give you constant reminders to use good manners. One of the most popular phrases in a growing family is, "Say thank you!" There's a reason why parents want to teach the lesson of showing gratitude. When was the last time you thanked God for all that he's done for you? Our Father in heaven wants to know you are thankful for your many blessings. Even Jonah, sitting in the stinky, dark belly of a giant fish, showed his gratitude to the Lord. If Jonah can be thankful from the pit of a fish, we can be thankful for all that we have.

Thank you, God, for the numerous blessings that surround me every day. Thank you for your salvation and your provision. Thank you for the family of believers I have known and for the ways in which you bless them.

Result of Righteousness

The result of righteousness will be peace;
the effect of righteousness
will be quiet confidence forever.

ISAIAH 32:17 CSB

The righteous delight in God's law and meditate on it day and night. They prosper in all they do, are morally excellent, and never listen to the advice of the wicked. Yet God's Word also says there are none that are righteous, so how will we find peace? The answer is Jesus. When we place our faith in Christ, his righteousness becomes our righteousness because we are filled with his Spirit. Once we belong to Jesus, we are sealed, and nothing can come between us and the promises of our God.

God, why do I choose trouble when peace is so simple to find? Fill me with your Spirit today, sanctifying me in purity and making me a bringer of peace. I do not want wickedness, and I do not want sin. I want you, and I desire your peace.

Simple Pleasures

I've learned from my experience
that God protects the vulnerable.
For I was broken and brought low,
but he answered me and came to my rescue!

PSALM 116:6 TPT

In a dangerous situation, would it be your instinct to protect a child or a soldier? It's impossible to imagine pushing past a little one to throw ourselves in front of someone armed and prepared. We go where we are needed. So it is with the Lord. The more confident we are in our own ability and the less vulnerable we are before him, the less of his protection he offers. He isn't offended by us; he just won't force himself on us. When we do cry to him, humble and helpless, we can be sure he will come to our rescue.

Lord, you will surely defend yourself. When man stands proud and proclaims himself sovereign, you will not be offended for long. You will surely declare your power and show the world who created all things.

Sing to the King

Sing praises to God, sing praises!
Sing praises to our King, sing praises!

PSALM 47:6 NKJV

We may not all have the voice of an angel, but we can all sing—no matter how good or bad it sounds to us. God created us each with a voice and with lips that can praise him for all the good things he has done. God is the King of the earth and the King of our hearts. He will delight in our songs of praise even if he is the only one who appreciates them. We should sing praises to God because we understand his goodness and grace. We should sing because he is worthy.

How great are you, Lord God Almighty! You have reached down from your perfect comfort in heaven to help the wretched and despised and make the foolish wise and the weak strong. You have brought glory to your name by your many great works.

Skilled

I will tell everyone about your righteousness.
All day long I will proclaim your saving power,
though I am not skilled with words.

PSALM 71:15 NLT

Very rarely do we find a person skilled at something they did not practice. Few are naturally skilled, and for those who are, likely they had some early developmental advances that benefited them. No man can boast in himself because even the practiced expert probably received his determination and focus from his parents. Time and time again we see winners, experts in their fields, honor God. Ultimately the abilities and proficiencies we develop come from him. We are made in his image and for his praise.

Lord, I am not a man of great talent, but I know that you often choose to be glorified through the weak and foolish. If I need any strength for your purpose, please give it to me, and I will give you the glory for it.

Skillfully Made

You formed my inward parts;
you knitted me together in my mother's womb.

PSALM 139:13 ESV

Think of a project you've done. Maybe you strung words together into works of art, carefully pieced together a quilt, or faithfully tended to a garden. Perhaps you've poured your time and heart into a career. Whatever you've set your hands to, think about how you feel about what you've created. It's a part of you. It houses your energy, your sacrifice, your creativity, and your hard work. It is of great value to you. It's yours. On the days you feel unloved or undervalued, remember the value of that work and think of how it only dimly mirrors God's feeling toward you. He has knit you together, faithfully and diligently, and you are of great value to him because you are his.

You saw me before the earth came to be. You knew my every vein and every bone before man knew how to speak. You have loved me for millennia. I stand amazed at your care and love, unrivaled and incomprehensible.

Sleep Life a King

> That night the king could not sleep; so he ordered the book
> of the chronicles, the record of his reign, to be brought in
> and read to him.
>
> ESTHER 6:1 NIV

Some nights we collapse into bed. Other nights it's a long, delicious process of winding down and letting the day's busyness melt away. You may have a bedtime routine which helps you relax—a book, a hot bath, or a nice cup of chamomile tea. God uses even sleepless nights for his purposes. Can it be God has your eyes open and mind alert for an unseen reason? Perhaps someone needs intercession, and you are awake for that purpose. Your prayer may prove to be part of a much greater plan.

Lord, please help me to see the working of your will in the ordinary and in the mundane things of life. Show me how I can serve you with the sleepless nights, the traffic jams, and the time spent waiting in lines.

So Much Love

As they stoned him, Stephen prayed, "Lord Jesus, receive my spirit." He fell to his knees, shouting, "Lord, don't charge them with this sin!" And with that, he died.

ACTS 7:59-60 NLT

If someone were throwing stones at you, would you just stand there and pray for them? Probably not! But that's what Stephen in the Bible did. He knew that the people who were hurting him did not really understand God. Stephen forgave them for hurting him. Have you been hurt by people before? Take some time today to forgive them. Tell Jesus that you want these people to know his love.

What a thing it is to love the unloved, Lord! I pray that I would count it an honor to love someone who shows no love toward me. Please take me and make me an unbreakable vessel of your compassion.

Everything Beyond

Praise him, sun and moon,
praise him, all you shining stars!

PSALM 148:3 ESV

It is amazing enough that the Lord made the earth and everything in it, from the blade of grass to the scurrying ant. Even more amazing is that he created the heavens, the universe, and everything beyond that. In their own way, all of these living things praise the Lord. The sun reflects his glory, the moon his mystery, and the stars his infinite being. As you rise with the sun this morning, think of your own way to honor your Creator.

Lord, may I every day discover a new way to honor you. I am your son, and you are my Father. You have chosen me from among the nations to spread your fame and shout your name, and I will not forget this!

Speak Well

"I hope I continue to please you, sir," she replied.
"You have comforted me by speaking so kindly to me,
even though I am not one of your workers."

RUTH 2:13 NLT

It's hard to feel good about yourself in a world full of
comparisons and awards for being the best at something.
While we don't want to waste our skills and talents, we also
don't want to focus on using them to show that we are the
best. We want to use them for the benefit of others! We
should be praising those who are doing well because they
can use their gifts to help better the world. Think of someone
you admire, or are even envious of, and instead of trying to
expose a weakness, praise their strength.

*God, I thank you for the skills and strengths that others
have, and I do not. I thank you that I am not the best at
everything imaginable. May the joy and victories of others
bring me joy just as easily as my own success.*

Spiritual Achievement

Everything that was written in the past was written to teach us. The Scriptures give us patience and encouragement so that we can have hope.

ROMANS 15:4 NCV

Ask most believers how to grow in faith and they will answer: read your Bible, pray, and go to church. So why is it so hard for us to open our Bibles? Do we truly believe it matters? Maybe it is a nagging feeling that time spent reading the ancient text is not productive. Perhaps we tend to trust popular speakers, pastors, or authors instead of trusting that the Holy Spirit speaks to us. We have an enemy who will do anything to keep us from the hope found in God's Word. Make it a necessity and your lifeline, not a book of suggestions you turn to occasionally. It will make a difference.

Dear Jesus, your Word is a lamp for my feet and bread for my soul. Why is it so hard for me to prioritize it? Show me the glory of having your Scripture within grasp and teach me to appreciate it more than gold.

Stand Victorious

I have saved these most important truths for last: Be
supernaturally infused with strength through your life-union
with the Lord Jesus. Stand victorious with the force of his
explosive power flowing in and through you.

EPHESIANS 6:10 TPT

Every day, we engage in spiritual battles. They are so real
and important that Paul saved some important tactics for
overcoming them until the end of his letter. Our strength
is supernatural because it comes from the Lord. We do not
have the power or strength to overcome sin and darkness by
ourselves. With the light of Christ in us, the victory is ours,
and nothing can bring us down. God is standing near, ready
to give us everything we need to overcome.

*With a broken body and a hoarse voice, your praises still
ring through my soul! You are a God of victories, and I count
the tribulation I face in your name as a victor's crown of
glory, beyond all earthly value.*

Stormy Weather

Suddenly a furious storm came up on the lake so that the
waves swept over the boat. But Jesus was sleeping.

MATTHEW 8:24 NIV

Have you ever been in a deep sleep and then been jolted
awake by a boom of thunder or a bright bolt of lightning? It's
an instant awakening, and then it's often impossible to get
back to sleep. Sometimes the storms of life roll into our homes
with the power of those intense booms and flashes outside.
We're hit by howling winds of adversity. Those are the times
that it's hard to have a grateful heart, but God wants us to
praise him in the storm. Even when we don't understand, we
can trust him to hold us close and keep us safe.

*Why did you sleep, Jesus? Help me to be of the same mind,
steadfast in faith and peaceful because of it. As long as I
trust in you and devote my life to knowing your grace, how
could my life ever be in jeopardy?*

Stretched Out

I lift my hands to you in prayer.
As a dry land needs rain, I thirst for you.

PSALM 143:6 NCV

Praying doesn't always make your pain go away, but it can meet your greater needs. David says, "I lift my hands to you." He is asking God to make sense and meaning out his circumstances. He says, "I thirst for you like a dry land needs rain." He needs to be filled with God before addressing his plight. We ask for God to be present with us. His expression of love is like a parent-child embrace, where we are fully encompassed by him through our pain and frustration.

Refresh me, God of healing. Fill up my empty soul, quench my thirsty heart. Within me there is a deep longing for your presence, and I know that you can give it to me. Be nearer to me than I could ever know.

December

The LORD is close to everyone
who prays to him,
to all who truly pray to him.

PSALM 145:18 NCV

Stubbornly Redeemed

Therefore, my dear brothers and sisters, stand firm.
Let nothing move you.

1 CORINTHIANS 15:58 NIV

No one enjoys teaching a stubborn child. But stubbornness redeemed is commitment. In our lives, we can be like stubborn children, opposing the will of God and demanding our own way. But we can also be redeemed—stubbornly devoted to following God and keeping our eyes from distractions along the way. Instead of being stubborn today, be stubbornly redeemed instead. Pray for strength to stand firm in what is right.

God, give me an emphatic devotion to your will that cannot be shaken. Make me stubborn for the gospel, unwilling at any moment to let it be diminished or changed. By your pursuit of me I was saved, so I will continue to pursue you.

Sun Rising

"Because of the tender mercy of our God,
With which the Sunrise from on high will visit us,
To shine upon those who sit in darkness
and the shadow of death,
To guide our feet into the way of peace."

LUKE 1:78-79 NASB

What a beautiful description of the coming Messiah! At the time, there had been four hundred years of silence among the people of Israel. It was like living in a dark night. But now, with Jesus about to be born, the sun was rising. Have you ever watched the sunrise? Slowly, the blackness that engulfed you fades as brilliant colors welcome the dawn of a new day. This is how Jesus entered the world. No longer living in darkness or the shadow of death, we now see the light. Brilliant colors are all around because new life has come to us. Praise God!

Your brilliance surrounds me like a wind, God, and I am overcome by the incredible redemption of ordinary things. How is it that you loved a world with such mercy when it scorned you with such hatred?

Supporter

As we pray to our God and Father about you, we think of
your faithful work, your loving deeds, and the enduring
hope you have because of our Lord Jesus Christ.

1 THESSALONIANS 1:3 NLT

Everyone needs a support team. Recognition and the
support of others brings encouragement. Being a prayer
warrior for someone is one of the greatest gifts we can offer
a brother or sister in Christ. When we approach the throne
of grace for someone else, it gives that person peace and
hope. It can inspire them in times of difficulty, helping them
to push through and overcome. When we acknowledge
the service and love that another believer provides, we are
ultimately giving recognition and praise to Jesus, for it is he
who empowers and equips them in their actions.

*God, I pray that you would raise up a support network that
reminds me of your character. I also pray that I could be this
support for someone else. I want to be your hand reaching
into their life.*

Supporting Leaders

Be careful to live properly among your unbelieving neighbors. Then even if they accuse you of doing wrong, they will see your honorable behavior, and they will give honor to God when he judges the world.

1 Peter 2:12-14 NLT

Our leaders, politicians, and decision-makers are not all evil. We might only see the worst of people in power, but we also need to recognize that God can work in their hearts and that they need the grace of Jesus every bit as much as we do. We are full of our own pride, conceit, and opinions that might not even be right. Pray for your leaders. You don't have to agree with them, but you can honor them by asking God to grant them more integrity and the ability to lead more wisely.

Lord, I pray for those you have bestowed authority upon. It is a blessing, but it is also a burden to bear. I pray that they would bear it well, upholding the cause of the poor and needy and opposing the proud.

Teachable Spirit

Let the wise listen and add to their learning,
and let the discerning get guidance.

PROVERBS 1:5 NIV

What can you do if you find yourself with an unteachable spirit? You can change and grow in wisdom. The problem is pride. If you avoid accountability because you don't think anyone else knows better than you do, or you justify away your actions when confronted, that's pride. If you don't think you need God's Word for wisdom, and you spend hardly any time in it, that's pride. A proud heart does not like rebuke, it does not receive correction from God or from the people God uses. But all hope is not lost. You can pray today and ask God to forgive you of your pride. A teachable heart is essential to a life of deep meaning and joy.

Lord, please forgive me of my insidious pride and renew within me a humble, contrite spirit. I need you working within me, for without you I am lost and blinded by my own sin.

Tenant Farmers

We are here for only a moment, visitors and strangers in the land as our ancestors were before us. Our days on earth are like a passing shadow, gone so soon without a trace.

1 CHRONICLES 29:15 NLT

We live on land that really doesn't belong to us. We may hold the deed to the property, but we are just passing through this world on our way to a much better destination. We are working for the Master of the land for his benefit. We even get to play with his other children while we are here. God has entrusted his beautiful world to us. Let's double our efforts and be the best tenant farmers we can be. Let's take time to enjoy the land he's given us. Let's praise God and give him the glory for the creation that he allows us to enjoy.

I am like a blade of grass which springs to life and grows older in just a few days. You are eternal, Lord, unable to be contained and without end. May the whole earth praise your name this day, glorifying you as its Creator.

Breed Joy

Give thanks for everything to God the Father
in the name of our Lord Jesus Christ.

EPHESIANS 5:20 NLT

Thankfulness breeds joy. Thankfulness extinguishes bitterness and comparison. It can move you out of self-centeredness and shift your focus onto what is good. Sometimes, walking in thanksgiving is incredibly hard, but don't let that keep you from doing it. Deliberately choose to be thankful. Let God soften your heart as you humbly take notice of what is good in your life. Whether it is a little or a lot, obvious or hidden, there are always reasons to praise him.

Blessed be your name, El Shaddai, Yahweh, Lord above all. Whether in tribulation or in comfort, I will praise you for the promise of heaven ahead of me and my past which you graciously redeemed.

Thankful for Life

Enter his gates with thanksgiving;
go into his courts with praise.
Give thanks to him and praise his name.

PSALM 100:4 NLT

This verse isn't just a figurative poetic song. It's based on the way the Israelites used to commune with God. They were to walk into his courts with a heart of gratitude. That's how we should approach God as well. You may wake up with a heavy heart, feeling like you want to give up on your day. Instead, you can choose to thank God—for his provision, for his love, for the life he gave you. If you do that, whether you feel like it or not, you'll soon find that your heart feels lighter.

My lungs open and close because you breathe life into all things. Thank you, Lord, for the grace your gospel has shown me and for the grace of my very existence. May I sing your praises today with newfound energy.

Final Kingdom

"You saw a stone break off from the mountain without a hand touching it, and it crushed the iron, bronze, fired clay, silver, and gold. The great God has told the king what will happen in the future. The dream is certain, and its interpretation reliable."

DANIEL 2:45 CSB

When Israel pictured an eternal kingdom, they were thinking of a physical kingdom, something like they had known but stronger and more powerful. God, however, had a plan that was beyond a kingdom made with human hands. His kingdom was not made from iron, bronze, clay, silver, or gold, but in the person of Jesus Christ, who started a kingdom that could never be destroyed. Remember that this is the kingdom you are a part of and praise God that the best is yet to come.

Father in heaven, may your kingdom come. May it storm the gates of every city, break down the walls of every human heart, and make your name known throughout the nations.

First Thing

I wake up early in the morning and cry out.
I hope in your word.

PSALM 119:147 NCV

How we end our day is just as important as how we begin it. If we fall asleep to late-night television, how likely are we to wake with thoughts of the Savior? If we drift off with our smartphones still in hand, might they be the first thing we reach for as we wake? Instead, let us find sleep while seeking the Father.

Father, you own every second of my day, buy may I learn to consecrate its beginning and end especially to you. May these periods of the day come to be my time spent alone with you.

Great Mystery

Oh, the depth of the riches, both of the wisdom and
knowledge of God! How unsearchable are His judgments
and unfathomable His ways!

ROMANS 11:33 NASB

God desires a relationship with us—a space where we
communicate our hearts and listen for his response. There
is so much to be gained from the knowledge of God. He is
beyond our human comprehension and sometimes so very
mysterious. But in all of the mystery, there is sovereignty and
love. When you're seeking wisdom, seek out God.

*God, I am at a loss, and I need your help. The path ahead
feels unsure, and my mind is not suitable for the decisions
ahead of me. Please help me to see where your plan is
leading me and how I can follow it faithfully.*

Hand Off

Commit to the LORD whatever you do,
and he will establish your plans.
PROVERBS 16:3 NIV

Prayer is bringing our requests to God and then handing them off. He picks up where we leave off, so we don't need to worry anymore. We commit things to him, trusting that he knows best. That's our part. His part is to establish our plans or answer our prayers. The problem comes when we try to do both our part and his. Unless we truly commit our way to the Lord, we won't allow him to work out his plan for us.

Establish my plans, Lord. I know that without you they will fail. Today I commit to you all my needs, hopes, and fears, and I pray that you would lay before me a clear path.

The Lord Hears

The righteous cry out, and the LORD hears,
And delivers them out of all their troubles.

PSALM 34:17 NKJV

Troubles are an unavoidable part of life in this fallen world. We are not exempt from them simply because we are believers in Jesus. Our deliverer is the living, all-powerful God who is present with us. In Jesus, we have an advocate who stands before the Father at all times. He hears our heart's cry and wants to come to our aid. He is big enough to handle our honesty when we share how we feel with him. Consider the privilege and blessing of having the eager, listening ear of your Savior at any moment.

Lord, I have been low, and I have been raised up high. I have seen your faithful hand leading me. When I have cried out in the desperation of my soul, you have always rescued me in your time. It has not always been what I expected, but your rescue has always come. Thank you.

He Sees Me

All my longings lie open before you, LORD;
my sighing is not hidden from you.
PSALM 38:9 NIV

Unlike empty promises in our pasts or people who disappointed us, God hears us and responds. Perhaps his responses are not what we expected or hoped for, but they are always loving and perfect. When we are at our most vulnerable and broken, he offers relief and comfort. He does not always remove us from our trials, but he takes our hands and guides us through them. He holds us when we cry. He collects our tears and remembers every one of our hurts. Nothing escapes his notice, and he cares deeply and intimately for each and every one of us.

Like a mother holding her child as his tears flow freely, please hold me, Jesus. Hold me close, and don't let me go from your embrace. This life is not easy; it is impossible on my own, so don't let go.

More Important One

Love is patient and kind.
Love is not jealous, it does not brag,
and it is not proud.

1 CORINTHIANS 13:4 NCV

There's something built inside us that makes us want to brag: "Look what I did!" But what if we spent more time bragging about others than we did about ourselves? That would show a special kind of love and honor. When we pay attention to others, it means we're taking our eyes off ourselves. Love is patient and kind. It's about giving up our own will for someone we love more.

Lord, I pray that you would create in me true love. May it be a love that is sincere, patient, and without ulterior motive. God, please make me a vessel of this love for those who need it most, and may it bring you glory.

Power of a Name

"In his name the nations will put their hope."

MATTHEW 12:21 NIV

Golden arches. Swoosh. Apple. What comes to mind with these words is more than what the word means: it's everything the word has come to represent. The same thing is true for the name of Jesus. That name means more than a name like Jacob or Sam or Peter. It stands for everything Jesus is and everything he has done. Jesus' name has power. Calling on that name and praying in it makes things happen.

All my hope is in you, Lord, all my faith is in you. Your name is power over darkness and faithfulness in uncertainty. Today, may your name be the reason I give for the hope that is within me.

Storyteller

Let the redeemed of the LORD
tell their story.

PSALM 107:2 NIV

Going to the mailbox at this time of year is an exciting adventure. You never know what you're going to get. When you open the mailbox and see all those white envelopes holding Christmas cards, it's thrilling to rip them open, gaze at the pictures, and read the letters. We all have a story to tell: a creative, intricate story designed just for us by the one who determines our steps. Your story is beautifully yours and one that should be nurtured and cherished every step of the way.

God, when I look back across my life, I see a life washed in redemption. All the sin and mistakes are washed clean, and your love has slowly been changing me from a selfish man of sin into one of grace.

Waiting Principle

The LORD must wait for you to come to him,
so he can show you his love and compassion.
For the LORD is a faithful God.
Blessed are those who wait for his help.

ISAIAH 30:18 NLT

In seasons of waiting, do you continue to press into the presence of God? Do you ask him for what you do not have? Do you rely on his help to persevere through hardship and trial? God's love is stronger than the grave, and he will not neglect to cover you with the power of his mercy whenever you come to him. Trust him. Continue to pray, ask, and seek. Wait on his help. He will not let you down.

Jesus, I will not cease to seek your face. When the darkness presses in all around, and I am pushed down by life, I will continue to place my requests before you day and night. I desire to hear your voice.

Will of God

> "Father, if you are willing, remove this cup from me.
> Nevertheless, not my will, but yours, be done."
>
> LUKE 22:42 ESV

Jesus left us a perfect example of submission to God's will when he was in the garden of Gethsemane, just prior to his crucifixion. How can we begin to fathom how it felt to accept that fate on our behalf? It was so difficult and painful for him that he sweated drops of blood! Still, he said, "Not my will, but yours be done." As believers, we are invited to surrender to God's will, even when it is contrary to what we desire. Even when it hurts, God's will is always perfect and always good. Let us remember that the grace of God is sufficient to carry us through anything.

God, how am I to bear this burden? My back is breaking, and I find no sympathy in the eyes of this world. If I am to endure this, then please sustain me and make me last longer than the trial.

Time to Rest

Let my soul be at rest again,
for the LORD has been good to me.

PSALM 116:7 NLT

There are so many things to do in a day! Go to work, hang out with friends, attend a small group, talk to family. Being excited for things is good, but we also want to take time to rest. There is a reason that we have to sleep each night. It may seem like you have too much to do to sleep, but without it, your body cannot function properly. God calls us to rest. He wants us to rest our bodies, hearts, and minds. Sit down for a few minutes and think about him. Take a little time to rest with God today.

Now is a time to rest. God, I know that I can rest in your peace because you are watching out for me. I will not be surprised and uprooted but will be guarded by your great and outstretched arm.

Transformed by Renewal

Let the Spirit renew your thoughts and attitudes.

EPHESIANS 4:23 NLT

We are bombarded daily with messages, texts, and social media comments. When we read the news on the disturbing conditions of our world, or view posts that cause us to believe the grass is greener on the other side, it can negatively alter our mood. When this infects us, it also affects our family, friends, and work environment. God's provision for this situation is his Holy Spirit. When we get alone with God in prayer, letting his Spirit dwell within us, quiet us, and soothe us, our outlook and demeanor change. We start to adopt God's perspective. Let him transform your mind today.

God, I am broken and malformed. My mind is riddled with cynicism, fear, and addictions. With you, there is hope for transformation, so please be at work in me in a new way.

Unending Blessings

Surely you have granted him unending blessings
and made him glad with the joy of your presence.

PSALM 21:6 NIV

David penned the beginning of this psalm of praise while looking back over experiences he had with the Lord. We can turn our experiences into praise as well with the gift of hindsight. Where have you seen God come through for you in faithfulness? Where has he deposited blessings in your life? You are living in the outpouring of his love. Even when you walk through valleys where it is hard to see and the shadows grow long, his mercy is with you as you journey. Be encouraged in the incomparable goodness of his presence and the promise of his continued faithfulness.

All around me is the testimony of your faithfulness, God. I feel the breeze, I see the ground beneath my feet, and I know that you are not done with this place. Thank you, God! May your name be lifted up this day.

Carrying the Story

The angel said to them, "Don't be afraid, for look, I proclaim to you good news of great joy that will be for all the people. Today in the city of David a Savior was born for you, who is the Messiah, the Lord."

LUKE 2:10-11 CSB

You will probably celebrate Christmas with some manner of tradition. Whatever the traditions are, you probably hold them very near to your heart and hope they will last as time goes on. Have you ever felt lost in all the tradition and wondered if Jesus is truly being celebrated? It's easy to feel disappointed when we forget to elevate Jesus. But remember, our celebration of Christmas actually serves the purpose of carrying the story of Good News forward!

Dear Jesus, thank you for coming in the form of an infant to conquer death and establish your kingdom! Thank you for living your earthly life, filled with pain and mockery, so I might know the love of the Father.

Peace Is Here

"Glory to God in the highest,
and on earth peace among those with whom he is pleased!"
LUKE 2:14 ESV

What a wonderful season to celebrate both the glory of God and the peace he offers. As we remember the glorious mystery of Jesus, the God man who humbled himself to be born a helpless baby and raised in the limits of flesh and bones, may we also remember the great gift of peace with God. There is no more striving for perfection according to the Law. Mercy's law has been perfected through the life, death, and resurrection of Jesus Christ. He is our holy hope. Let us lift our unrestrained worship to him today. Let us glorify his great and holy name, for he is our peace.

Jesus Christ, how perfect is your name! May it be sung and heard to the ends of the age. I pray that everyone would come to know it as a sound of redemption and healing: the proclamation of Immanuel.

Importance

Unto us a Child is born, unto us a Son is given; and the government will be upon His shoulder. And His name will be called Wonderful, Counselor, Mighty God, Everlasting Father, Prince of Peace.

ISAIAH 9:6 NKJV

"Happy Birthday, Jesus!" the family exclaimed. They all put aside the materialism of Christmas, placing their focus on the birth of their Savior. They still had a tree and a few presents, but they decided not to follow the world or the commercialization of the day. There was no hustle and bustle, but there was a birthday cake, songs of praise, and the presence of the Savior as they honored his coming to earth for mankind. As you celebrate the birth of Christ, remember that he is the greatest gift of all.

How precious it is to be adopted into your family, Lord! I was an orphan in the spirit, yet you chose to bring me in. You chose to live the life I could not, so I might have your righteousness and wear your royal robes.

Unending Chorus

Creation itself will be set free from its bondage to corruption
and obtain the freedom of the glory of the children of God

ROMANS 8:21 ESV

Some days begin with praises on our lips and a song to God
in our hearts. Humility covers us like a velvet cloth, soothing
and delicate and gentle. The truth of God plays on repeat,
and the entire world's darkness cannot interrupt its chorus.
Other days begin by fumbling with the snooze button and
forfeiting the chance to meet him in the stillness. The ups
and downs should be familiar by now, but can we ever
become accustomed to the holy living side-by-side with our
flesh? One glorious day, flesh will give way to freedom, and
only holy will remain. This leaves praise on our lips and a
song in our hearts—an unending chorus of his goodness!

*God, I pray that my mind and heart would be conditioned
to desiring your will. May the comfort of this life be nothing
to me in comparison to the joy of bringing your love to the
unloved and brokenhearted!*

Unlimited Resources

I pray that from his glorious, unlimited resources he will
empTEXT empower you with inner strength through his Spirit.

EPHESIANS 3:16 NLT

Paul prayed that the love of Christ would overflow in the
readers of his letter. He asked that the unlimited resources of
Christ's kingdom would empower them with inner strength.
You can know the glorious hope of the God who has called
you his own. You are a part of his kingdom and a co-heir
with Christ. May you be filled with all you need, and more
than you can imagine, in fellowship with his Spirit. Be
blessed today.

*God, I pray for your inner strength to dwell within me. I
know these trials may not be over soon, but I pray that I
would not have to face them any longer without your power
and grace to meet them head on.*

Unwrap Grace

It was only through this wonderful grace that we believed in him. Nothing we did could ever earn this salvation, for it was the gracious gift from God that brought us to Christ! So no one will ever be able to boast, for salvation is never a reward for good works or human striving.

EPHESIANS 2:8-9

It's pretty annoying when you run into that one family member or friend that always has to outdo everyone. They love to boast about the things they are able to purchase and do, and though their charity isn't a bad thing, their attitude of bragging gives it a negative edge. Let's check ourselves. Are we Christians who speak as though the grace we have in our lives is a result of our own doing? Any grace we have, any blessing, is 100% the work of our Father in heaven. Let us be careful to give credit and praise where it is due and not try to obtain it for ourselves.

To you, my precious Savior, is all the glory due! In love and grace, you revived me from death and made me part of your plan. May my lips forever sing your praise, until my body can strive no longer and I am laid to rest.

Use Your Head

Trust in the LORD with all your heart
And do not lean on your own understanding.
PROVERBS 3:5 NASB

Using your head isn't such a bad idea to help you solve a problem. Sometimes the answer you're praying for is just a matter of good sense. While using common sense or your own understanding is a great idea, depending on it isn't. Talk about your problem and potential solution with a few others you trust. Most importantly, go to God and ask him what he thinks. Lean on his understanding instead of your own, and you will always come out on top.

God, you are wise beyond all human understanding. Things may not make sense to me, but I know that they are clear to you. Even the night is as day in your eyes. Make my way clear and prepare a path ahead of me.

What to Do

If the foundations are destroyed,
what can the righteous do?

PSALM 11:3 ESV

Often we try our very hardest and still don't get the outcome
that we were hoping for. You might try to make a right
decision in your workplace, yet the project still falls apart.
You might think you have dealt fairly with your children, but
they still grumble and complain. Perhaps you followed the
rulebook on the right diet and still don't feel any healthier.
What do the righteous do when the foundations of what
should work, don't? You might never get your answer, but
you can pray that you find peace in the knowledge that the
mystery of God's ways will one day be revealed.

*Lord, you are glorified when I am at a loss of understanding.
The confusion and the distress remind me that you are God,
and I am not. Your ways transcend mine, so please give me
faith to endure the trial.*

Praise Party

Praise the LORD!
Praise God in his sanctuary;
praise him in his mighty heaven!

PSALM 150:1 NLT

The end of the year should be a celebration whether it has been a good year or a difficult one. Take some time to reflect on what your hopes were for this year and allow yourself to mourn the things that didn't go as planned. Let go of that disappointment and ask God to heal the grief. Turn your thoughts toward all the wonderful things that you were a part of or that you achieved on your own. Thank God for graciously guiding you through it all. Then celebrate a year that has come to an end and the new hope that begins when you awake tomorrow.

God, I thank you for this year and for all it has brought. May it be a source of reflection and testimony, and may I learn to glorify you for both the joys and the pains. Take this next year and make it a season for your praise to increase in the earth.